CATHOLIC AND LOVING IT

D0167685

CATHOLIC AND LOVING IT

TRADITIONS FOR A NEW GENERATION

**Andrew Salzmann
and Sabitha Narendran**

PUBLISHED BY ST. ANTHONY MESSENGER PRESS
CINCINNATI, OHIO

Library of Congress Cataloging-in-Publication Data

Salzmann, Andrew.
  Catholic and loving it : traditions for a new generation / Andrew
Salzmann and Sabitha Narendran.
      p. cm.
  Includes bibliographical references.
  ISBN 978-0-86716-807-5 (pbk. : alk. paper) 1. Catholic Church. 2. Church
year. I. Narendran, Sabitha. II. Title.

BX1754.S274 2007
282—dc22

                            2007010486

ISBN 978-0-86716-807-5

Published by Servant Books, an imprint of
St. Anthony Messenger Press.
28 W. Liberty St.
Cincinnati, OH 45202
www.ServantBooks.org

Printed in the United States of America.
Printed on acid-free paper.

07 08 09 10 11 5 4 3 2 1

With gratitude

to Mary, Notre Dame, our mother, the model of faith
—JOHN 19:27

to our families, who raised us in households of faith
—GALATIANS 6:10

to John Paul II, who inspired in us a life of faith
—LUKE 22:32

Contents

Foreword

The LORD our God is one LORD; and you shall love the LORD your God with all your heart, and with all your soul, and with all your might. And these words which I command you this day shall be upon your heart; and you shall teach them diligently to your children, and shall talk of them when you sit in your house, and when you walk by the way, and when you lie down, and when you rise.

—DEUTERONOMY 6:4–7

On any given Sunday morning, in virtually every corner of the world, Catholics stream into their favorite pews for the eucharistic meal. God's Word and his own Body and Blood illuminate and nourish our souls amid smells and bells. Meanwhile vigil candles burn before the Mary and Joseph statues in silent intercession. Other saints, their images emblazoned in stained glass, challenge us to aspire to a higher level of holiness when we exit the church doors.

The well-known traditions within the Roman Catholic faith speak to a collective existence, uniting the body of Christ in a cultural way. Growing up Catholic involved certain understandings: scapulars though itchy were a must, statues adorned not only churches but also homes and gardens, holy days were obligatory days of Mass and festivity, and the saints were reliable intercessors for everything from sore throat relief to safe travel.

There is something beautiful about the collective Catholic existence. It's the comprehension that we are part of something far bigger than our immediate parish surroundings. The rituals and sacramentals of our faith are signs of a living Church, an organic collection of sinners all "straining forward to what lies ahead" (Philippians 3:13). There is meaning behind the feasts, fasts, medals and icons. A heavenly ear listens to each and every rosary and novena.

The fact that our Catholic faith is so old and so rich makes this book a natural accessory for Catholics young and old. Many of us learned the *what* but not the *why* of Catholic traditions and prayers in parochial schools and from devout parents and grandparents. Here, Sabitha Narendran and Andrew Salzmann seek to unpack and explain the depth and the breadth of God's love as encountered in these practices. Their personal experiences, solid research and sincere love for the Roman Catholic faith will inspire even the questioning heart.

The authors brought their rich Catholic heritage to Notre Dame with them and found a group of fellow students eager to share it. I wish I had had a book like theirs back in my dorm days. This is a great resource for the young, single Catholic who longs for a deeper Church experience.

Now that I'm married and have children, I see this book as a resource for bringing more life to my own "domestic Church." As a Catholic father I have undertaken far more than providing food, clothing and good schooling to my daughters. My vocation is steeped in their salvation: not to get them into Harvard but to get them into heaven. And not a day goes by that I don't thank God for the gift of his Church and its rich history and devotions that accompany the immeasurable gifts of the sacraments and the Scriptures. God freely gives these with the express purpose of helping us fulfill our call as Christians and as parents: "salvation of...souls" (1 Peter 1:9).

As you read through the following pages, you might be surprised to learn the history of various traditions. At other times you might nod, recalling lessons learned while clad in plaid in Catholic school. Most assuredly you will find yourself smiling at memories of beloved family members who exemplified devotion.

You probably will grow in appreciation for all those who have gone before us in the faith, especially those so in love with the Lord that they were inspired to seek new expressions to help others enter into God's mysterious love more fully. My hope is that you find among the practices here some that you can implement. Our goal is to live the faith, and books like this one make it simpler and a whole lot more fun.

Mark Hart
Author, *Blessed Are the Bored in Spirit:
A Young Catholic's Search for Meaning*

Catholic and Loving It

We are under no illusions that our college experience was normal. Sabitha came from Houston to pursue a degree in architecture; Andrew was a theology student from Wisconsin. At the University of Notre Dame we, and a couple dozen others, formed a group dedicated to living a life in Christ and to living it abundantly (see John 10:10).

The campus of Notre Dame was perhaps the perfect environment for all this, though even there our experience wasn't quite typical. We said the rosary together around St. Mary's Lake, under warm stars and freezing snow. We shared our complaints and our successes with God each day at Mass and with each other right after. We organized processions, celebrated patron saint feast days and sang the *Regina Coeli* in the dining hall. The life we began there—celebrating Christ with the traditions of an ancient, global Church—was a beautiful life in which God became ever more completely "the joy of our youth."

CULTURES OF FAITH

Sixty years ago Catholics in America celebrated the passing of the week, the day, the whole year, with myriad customs. Growing up in Marathon City, Wisconsin, Andrew's grandfather looked forward to the visit of Saint Nicholas to enliven a harsh winter. Children spent summers living in the convent as they prepared for First Communion. Processions through farm fields implored God's blessing on the crops. And the annual Corpus Christi celebration was, according to Aunt Adeline, something "to look forward to when we didn't have much else during the Depression."

Jesus, too, was born into an intensely liturgical environment. National life centered on the temple, where rites and ceremonies marked the passing of the times of day and year (see Numbers 28—29; Leviticus 25:10). Jewish life centered particularly on the covenant made at Sinai, the Mosaic Law (the code of conduct that maintained the Israelite presence in that covenant) and the ritual celebration of Passover at the family and national levels (see Exodus 12). Scholars are finding that the Bible itself was written to be a sort of lectionary, a liturgical book.[1]

Religiosity went beyond the official rites of the temple: Daily life was marked by expressions of personal commitment and devotion to God not required by the covenant.[2] Old women kept vigil with the presence of God in the temple (see Luke 2:36–38). People sought ritual washings in holy waters (John 5:2–3). The faithful prayed, repeating psalms and traditional Jewish prayers (see Matthew 21:9, Mark 15:34). Pilgrims traveled to holy sites (Luke 2:41). Feasts and celebrations marked important events (John 2:1–10). Associations of the faithful came together for fasting, prayer and study (Matthew 9:14). Sound familiar?

This popular piety served the Jewish people well. With the destruction of the temple and the Diaspora, the national liturgy of Israel disappeared. Yet liturgy at the family level, like the seder meal, and popular religious practices helped the Jews retain a strong sense of self-identity, continuing as a people without a nation in the face of strong impulses to assimilate.[3]

The first Christians, and our Lord himself, inherited this world of popular religiosity. We should not be surprised then that Christians naturally sought expressions for their faith beyond what the liturgy and the new covenant require. Saint Paul's writings indicate that early Christians continued observing Jewish feasts, though the apostle warned them not to become slaves to these customs (see Galatians 4:8–11; Colossians 2:16). Paul appears to have observed Passover and Pentecost, and the First Letter to the Corinthians may contain the earliest recorded Easter homily (1 Corinthians 5:7–8; 16:8).[4] Very rapidly, Christians developed the most basic customs of funeral rituals, commemorations of martyrs and annual or weekly feasts and fasts, among others.

COMING TO AMERICA

The discovery and exploration of America were distinctly Catholic endeavors. Christopher Columbus held the conversion of the native peoples in the New World as one of the primary objects of his undertaking. Later missionaries worked in South America, the California coast and the Canadian wilderness.

Perhaps the one place in America where the Catholic Church was not active from the beginning was along the Atlantic coast. In the thirteen British colonies, fear and suspicion of Catholics continued from the era of the Reformation. As Catholics began immigrating to the young United States from Ireland, Germany, Poland, Italy and beyond, they faced prejudice, ridicule and economic hardship. Anti-Catholic propaganda induced a rash violence, most famously the burning of a Charleston convent in 1834. Political parties were established to quell Catholic immigration.[5]

In response, Catholics created their own institutions and subculture to care for themselves. In time they came to enjoy economic prosperity, the result of their disciplined schools and the post–World War II G.I. Bill, which allowed many to attend college. With this prosperity came a move to the suburbs and away from the ethnic enclaves, with their old-world traditions and established parishes. On the verge of becoming accepted members of society, Catholics were eager to distance themselves from languages and customs that betrayed their difficult immigrant past. At the election of President John F. Kennedy in 1960, older Catholics who never had imagined they would feel so accepted in the United States broke into tears.

From 1962 to 1965 the Second Vatican Council, a watershed gathering of bishops, discussed the problems the Church was facing in the modern world. Following World War II, church participation in Europe fell drastically. One French bishop at the council begged the gathering to "understand the plight of pastors who were faced with situations in which the Church was considered moribund…[and implored] bishops who still enjoyed the security of large, docile congregations…not to close their hearts and eyes to the needs of those living in dechristianized areas."[6]

Pope John XXIII hoped that, by calling the council, the bishops would reassess the position of the Church in modernity in order to effectively present the gospel anew to the world. The center of the Church's life and worship, the liturgy, had been carefully "formulated for the most part at a time when an agricultural society was dominated by a monastic spirituality" and therefore had to be renewed so as to be more meaningful to modern, urban, de-Christianized society.[7]

The council initiated a path of reform intended to accommodate the Church's discipline and liturgy to the world of modern believers, assisting efforts at reevangelization. The steady stream of reforms, however, created an environment in which much of Catholic teaching and practice was in flux. Combined with the socioeconomic realities in the United States, a lot of popular piety disappeared from the American Church in this process of reform and assimilation.

TIME TO CELEBRATE

The Church still recognizes the value of popular piety. "Popular piety is the soul without which the liturgy cannot thrive," explains Pope Benedict. "Unfortunately…on the occasion of the postconciliar reform, it has frequently been held in contempt or even abused. Instead, one must love it, purifying and guiding it where necessary, but always accepting it with great reverence…as the dedicated sanctuary of faith in the hearts of the people."[8] The Second Vatican Council decreed that the "popular devotions of the Christian people are to be highly commended" and that they should be attuned to the liturgy, flowing from it and leading the people always back to it.[9]

Our little book hopes to further the call of the council by presenting the customs it praised in a way accessible to, well, modern believers. By extending the faith beyond the official, liturgical context, all of life can be "evangelized," the promise and love of Christ being spread to our whole lives.

Yet the value of popular piety goes beyond its benefit to the health of Christianity. Simply enjoying the presence of friends and family in the light of God is the only justification necessary. The instrument of God's glorification, believed Saint Irenaeus (d. 202), is the person who is grateful to his Creator.[10]

Our book then is not a recipe for forming devoted Catholics; that requires a strong relationship to our Lord. Nor is it a program to renew the Church; this we entrust to our leaders. Nor do we suggest that following everything in this book will, *ex opere operatus*, bring happiness; without spiritual fervor and prayer everything we recommend can become burdensome clutter and contrived ritual. Rather we offer ways to enjoy ourselves while living a life in Christ—in other words, to *celebrate* Christ.

During the Great Depression Solanus Casey, a Franciscan friar known for his innocent sanctity, began a soup kitchen to feed hungry workers near Detroit. Andrew's grandfather was among the many he fed in those years. It was in Michigan that the now Venerable Solanus Casey performed a rather remarkable miracle.

A woman had come into Father Casey's office with some ice cream cones to share, since it was a warm summer day. He thanked her but was overwhelmed with visitors and put them in his bottom desk drawer. She was understandably baffled by this behavior.

About three hours later, however, another friar entered the office. He had asked for Father Casey's prayers earlier in the day, before leaving for surgery, and had been healed on his way to the doctor. No surgery was necessary.

"Let's celebrate in honor of the Blessed Virgin!" rejoiced Father Casey. He went to his desk drawer and retrieved the ice cream cones, unmelted and perfectly cool. Looking at his friends, sharing their joy, the holy friar exclaimed, "It pleases Jesus and Mary greatly when we celebrate in this way."[11]

Chapter One

Catholic at Home

For the most part rural Wisconsin is filled with cows. Occasionally, though, you will come across a barn selling "antiques": old furniture, broken dolls, wagon wheels and—unless you're in a Lutheran town—a whole lot of Catholic memorabilia. Flowerpots shaped like Mary, dusty paintings of the Sacred Heart, porcelain statues of Saint Joseph—these people knew how to make a home look Catholic.

Of course, more than appearing Catholic, our homes must truly *be* Catholic: We must foster the spiritual environment that all this "Catholic paraphernalia" represents. Saint Paul summarizes that environment well: "Rejoice always, pray constantly, give thanks in all circumstances" (1 Thessalonians 5:16–18). With a spirit of joy and openness, the religious articles our forefathers embraced can meet their intended purpose of lifting our minds to God throughout the day.

THE HOME BLESSING

From the beginning Christianity has been a family-centered religion, with entire households being baptized together (see Acts 16:15). Our homes—our physical and emotional shelters—are the centers of our families, where we eat, sleep and live together. These should be dedicated to the service of

God, as a testament that "as for me and my house, we will serve the Lord" (Joshua 24:15).

As Sabitha grew up, a priest blessed every home the family occupied. Having a home blessed is easier than it may seem. Simply call your pastor and ask: We've never heard a priest decline. He will walk through each room, praying and blessing home and family with holy water. The blessing is in the Church's *Book of Blessings*, which the priest will supply. It takes thirty to forty-five minutes.

This is a good opportunity to get to know your pastor better. You might ask him to stay for lunch or dinner or a full-fledged party.

ENTHRONEMENT OF THE SACRED HEART

Inspired by the encouragement of the sisters teaching at their school, in 1950 Andrew's aunts and uncle saved up their money and purchased a large, framed image of the Sacred Heart for their home. The Church promoted the enthronement of the Sacred Heart to further dedicate households to Christ, recalling the promise of our Lord to Saint Margaret Mary Alacoque: "I will bless every place where a picture of My Heart shall be set up and honored."[1]

The Sacred Heart is "enthroned" when a suitably sized image is hung in a prominent place at the center of the family's daily activity. The ceremony can involve a priestly blessing but hinges upon the family's own commitment to honor Christ in their hearts and home. The enthronement is not a passing ceremony but a way of life.

Order of Enthronement of the Sacred Heart (*Roman Ritual*, Appendix)[2]

Priest: Our help is in the name of the Lord.

All: Who made heaven and earth.

Priest: Lord, heed my prayer.

All: And let my cry be heard by you.

Priest: The Lord be with you.

All: May he also be with you.

Priest: Let us pray. Hear us, holy Lord and Father, almighty everlasting God, and in your goodness send your holy angel from heaven to watch over and protect all who live in this home, to be with them and give them comfort and encouragement; through Christ our Lord.

All: Amen.

Priest: Let us pray. Lord Jesus Christ, as I, in all humility, enter this home, let there enter with me abiding happiness and God's choicest blessings. Let serene joy pervade this home and charity abound here and health never fail. Let no evil spirits approach this place but drive them far away. Let your angels of peace take over and put down all wicked strife. Teach us, O Lord, to recognize the majesty of your holy name. Sanctify our humble visit and bless + what we are about to do; you who are holy, you who are kind, you who abide with the Father and the Holy Spirit forever and ever.

All: Amen.

Priest: Let us pray. Almighty everlasting God, who does not forbid us to carve or paint likenesses of your saints, in order that whenever we look at them with our bodily eyes we may call to mind their holy lives, and resolve to follow in their footsteps; may it please you to bless + and to hallow + this picture, which has been made in memory and honor of your only-begotten Son, our Lord Jesus Christ, and grant that all who in its presence pay devout homage to your only-begotten Son may by His merits obtain your grace in this life and everlasting glory in the life to come; through Christ our Lord.

All: Amen.

The image is sprinkled with holy water.

Priest: Lord Jesus Christ, we acknowledge you as King of the universe. All that has been made exists for your glory. Exercise over us your sovereign rights. We now renew the promises of our baptism; we again renounce Satan and all his works and attractions; we again promise to lead a truly Christian life. And in a very special way we undertake to bring about the triumph of your rights and the rights of your Church. Sacred Heart of Jesus, we offer you our poor actions to obtain that all men acknowledge your sacred kingly power. May the kingdom of your peace be firmly established throughout the world.

All: Amen.

Priest: Lord Jesus Christ, who, while you were subject to Mary and Joseph, sanctified family life by your unexcelled virtues; grant that we, aided by Mary and Joseph, may be inspired by the example of your holy family, and so attain the happiness of living with them in heaven. We ask this of you who live and reign forever and ever.

All: Amen.

Lastly the priest blesses the family:

May the blessing of almighty God, Father, Son, + and Holy Spirit, come upon you and remain with you forever.

All: Amen.

HOLY WATER FONTS

If you visit Italy, Mexico or Spain and stop in one of the many ceramics shops, you may encounter, next to the dishes and across the aisle from candlestick holders, the holy water font section. These fonts, handmade and colorfully decorated, are a world apart from the ones usually found in the United States. From their quality and their location next to all the other "essential" household goods, you can see the importance of the family holy water font in these cultures.

The earliest forms of holy water fonts were fountains in the atriums of ancient Christian basilicas. These fountains were used to wash before prayer, a custom Christians inherited from Jewish practice. Holy water was used to purify the Levites of their sins so that they would be worthy to worship the Lord (see Numbers 8:7).[3] The physical washing gradually became less important as the spiritual properties attributed to the water (blessed, since at least the fourth century) grew. Writers from the sixth century speak of the use of holy water to banish evil and enlighten souls; Christians in the ninth century attributed to holy water the ability to renew the effects of baptism.

The Church today blesses water as a sacramental, making it a prayer for the expulsion of diabolical influence and the remission of venial sins in Christ's name. We know that only God can forgive sins (see Mark 2:7), that "the Son of man has authority on earth to forgive sins" (Mark 2:10; see Luke 7:48) and that he entrusted to the Church the authority to grant or refuse forgiveness of sins (John 20:21–23). The Church extends Christ's forgiveness of serious (or "mortal") sins through the sacrament of penance alone (*CCC*, 1446). But as holy water renews the effects of baptism, minor ("venial") sins can be washed away by the Church's blessing. Therefore, the "spirituality" of holy water can be summed up in one early Greek inscription found on holy water fonts, "Wash not only thy face but thy iniquities," or in the psalm sung while sprinkling holy water, "Purge me with hyssop [a plant used to sprinkle liquid], and I shall be clean; / wash me, and I shall be whiter than snow" (Psalm 51:7).[4]

Finding a cheap font is easy. Finding one you would want to display in your home, however, requires time and a little money. Nice brass fonts, for example, can be found in the United States. But note, holy water is made with salt, so an impenetrable mineral residue will build up in your font unless you wash it on a regular basis.

Fonts are usually placed near a frequently used door into the home, so that family members might bless themselves as they come and go. Parents often bless children with holy water before sending them to bed.

Most churches have large metal containers of holy water in the vestibule, but you may need to ask your pastor for some. Should you unfortunately endure a holy water drought, custom dictates that holy water can be "stretched" with plain water, so long as true holy water continues to make up three-fourths of the solution at any given time. Frankly, it's easier just to ask Father for more.

WHY SACRAMENTALS?

Sacramentals are sacred signs or ceremonies instituted by the Church to pray for particular petitions in Christ's name. While the sacraments are the seven covenantal ceremonies at the center of Christianity, which Christ has promised will always be answered with an outpouring of grace, the sacramentals are an almost limitless collection of formal prayers that derive their power from simply being prayers of the whole Church, beseeching Christ to pour out the fruits of his saving passion, death and resurrection (see CCC, 1670). Through sacramentals the Church prays that an individual may receive the remission of venial sins, the blessing of daily endeavors, the gift of particular favors, healing, a lessening of diabolical influence or whatever else the whole chorus of saints in heaven might request before the throne of God Almighty.[5]

THE HOME ALTAR

"When you pray," instructs Our Lord, "go into your room and shut the door and pray to your Father who is in secret" (Matthew 6:6). The altar is such a place of private prayer: a quiet area of the home set aside—*consecratio*—as a place for the family to gather before God. If the Sacred Heart was enthroned in the middle of your busy home, the home altar should be in a quiet place, conducive to prayer. Though not a liturgical altar, it becomes the true altar of the *ecclesia domestica*, the "domestic Church," a name the Second Vatican Council gave to the Christian family.[6]

Thus, these altars are the center of "liturgy" for this domestic church. In Austrian homes, for example, the beginning of Advent is marked with a procession through the home with the crèche, which is finally laid on the family's altar. Join in harmony with the liturgy of the whole Church by using your altar to mark the passage of liturgical time.

Mentioned throughout the Old and New Testaments, an altar is, by definition, a table at which sacrifices and offerings are made to God. Most basically, your altar will consist of a table placed against the wall. If possible, you might place it against the eastern wall of your home: Churches are often built facing east, in anticipation of the Second Coming of the Son of God, the rising of the sun of righteousness (see Malachi 4:2). According to Russian folklore, evil spirits settle in corners, so personal oratories were often put in corners to dispel them.

Practically speaking, the table should be at a comfortable height for kneeling and large enough to hold the sacramentals you wish to place on it. Leave enough space around the altar for all to gather comfortably. If only one person will normally pray before the shrine, you might furnish a kneeler.

Your shrine can be quite simple or intrepidly complex, but it should be beautiful. Adorn it with sacramentals, including images of Christ and the saints, creating a recollected atmosphere that raises the heart to God. Consider the following:

- Crucifix. A simple cross simply won't do. In the words of Saint Paul, "We preach Christ *crucified*, a stumbling block to Jews and folly to Gentiles" (1 Corinthians 1:23, emphasis added). Crucifixes also are appropriate by the door of children's bedrooms and above a couple's bed.

- Bible. The imports store at the local mall sells stands on which you can place the Bible. If enshrining the Bible will make it less accessible, however, simply keep it near the altar: A Bible in pristine condition is a sad sight indeed.

- Missal(s). When the Mass was said in Latin, every Catholic had a missal for following the prayers of the liturgy during Mass. Even with vernacular liturgy, keeping a missal at home allows you to follow the liturgical season more closely.

- Paintings, Statues and Icons. Some image of Mary is a given in any home shrine: She is the mother and the model of all Christians (see John 19:27). Other suggestions include images of the family's patron saints and an image portraying the devotion of the month (see chapter two).

- Flowers. Votive offerings are mentioned no less than fourteen times in Sacred Scripture. Offering flowers to the Lord or his mother is a beautiful act of love.

- Cloths. Your altar will be much more attractive with some cloths. To express the liturgical season, consider using at least two: a longer cloth, hanging over the sides of the table, of the appropriate seasonal color and a shorter white cloth to cover the surface of the table.

- Blessed Candles. Two (or four or even six) blessed tapers might rest on the back of your altar, evenly divided between the left and the right sides of the altar and evenly spaced. These candles, ideally blessed on Candlemas, should be lit when the family gathers for prayer.

LITURGICAL COLORS

Green: Hope, the mark of "ordinary" Christian life
(Ordinary Time)

Violet: Penance, in preparation for Christmas and Easter
(Advent and Lent)

White: Innocence and triumph; see Revelation 3:5
(Christmas and Easter seasons)

Red: The blood of Christ and fire of the Spirit
(Passiontide and Pentecost)

Rose: It's not pink! Rejoicing
(Third Sunday of Advent and Fourth Sunday of Lent,
reminding us not to get carried away with sorrow)

Black: Sorrow and mourning
(optional for funerals and All Souls' Day)

Gold: For great feast days

WHY CANDLES?

The candle has rich symbolism. The *Exsultet,* sung at the Easter Vigil, compares the candle with Christ.

The Church exercises a preferential option for beeswax candles. This wax, born of the virgin "mother bee," symbolizes the *flesh* of Christ, born of the Virgin Mother.

The flame symbolizes the *divinity* of Christ, and the wick shows the seamless union of humanity and divinity in the *soul* of Christ. Just as lambs were burned as holocausts in the temple, the candle is a burnt offering that recalls the sacrifice of Jesus Christ, Lamb of God and Light of the World. To burn a candle in prayerful petition is an implicit act of asking in prayer "for the sake of his sorrowful passion."[7]

CATHOLICISM: DON'T LEAVE HOME WITHOUT IT

Now that your home is a den of piety, let us suggest some sacramentals for the road.

Catholic zeal for religious medals can be so impressive that we've heard one or two pilgrims coming before we actually saw them. This enthusiasm is ancient, dating at least to the second century. A medal from that time depicts Saints Peter and Paul.[8]

THE MIRACULOUS MEDAL

In June of 1830 a French nun, Catherine Labouré, began receiving visions of Our Lady under the title of her Immaculate Conception. Mary requested that a medal be struck, which finally happened after two years of discussion with Catherine's spiritual director and the archbishop. The medal Mary requested occasioned so many successful prayers for healing and conversion that it became known as "the Miraculous Medal."

Catherine spent the rest of her days as an ordinary nun. She is a canonized saint, and her feast day is November 28. Take that day to read up on her saintly life and to obtain a miraculous medal.

Originally Mary requested that the medals be struck in silver, but today you can find cheaper ones. You might want to have several medals blessed, then ask Father if you may

SYMBOLS OF SALVATION HISTORY ON THE MIRACULOUS MEDAL

Lettering around the edge	"O Mary, conceived without sin, pray for us who have recourse to thee."
Woman crushing a serpent	Mary, the Immaculate Conception (see Genesis 3:15)
Rays of light	The grace of God
Globe marked "1830"	The world, with the date of the apparition
Crown of twelve stars	The crown of Mary, Icon of the Church (Revelation 12:1)
Cross with the letter M	Mary at the foot of the cross (John 19:25)
Heart with a crown of thorns	The Sacred Heart of Jesus (Matthew 27:29)
Heart pierced by a sword	The Immaculate Heart of Mary (Luke 2:35)

leave some in the church for others. We passed them out once a semester in the cafeteria at Notre Dame, and the response was enthusiastic.

Saint Benedict Medal

The medal of Saint Benedict has been called one of the Church's most powerful sacramentals, dating back to at least 1415. The front of the medal has an image of Saint Benedict with a chalice and a raven, recalling a failed assassination attempt. The saint was given a poisoned meal, but when he made the Sign of the Cross in blessing over the food, the chalice of wine split in half, and the raven carried away the poisoned bread.

The reverse side of the medal contains the initials of some Latin phrases:

Crux sacra sit mihi lux! Nunquam draco sit mihi dux! May the holy cross be my light! May the dragon never be my guide!

Vade retro Satana! Nunquam suade mihi vana! Sunt mala quae libas. Ipse venena bibas! Begone, Satan! Never tempt me with your vanities! What you offer me is evil. Drink the poison yourself!

Crux Sancti Patris Benedicti: The cross of our holy father Benedict.

The medal's uses, of course, relate to these prayers and the prayers of the Church's blessing, which give the medal its efficacy. The verses relate to exorcism, and indeed the medal has been used as a means of repelling demonic influence throughout its history. Unto this end it is often worn around the neck, kept in a pocket, put into the foundations of houses and buildings, mounted on the walls of barns and sheds

WHY INDULGENCES?

Though talk of indulgences has faded in recent times, they are hard to avoid when writing a book about traditional Catholic practices. We know that Christ forgives sins through the sacrament of penance. So what does an indulgence do?

Reflecting on the expulsion of Adam and Eve from the Garden, we know that "it is a divinely revealed truth that sins bring punishments inflicted by God's sanctity and justice"[9] (see Genesis 3:16–19). Saint Paul therefore tells us to "judge ourselves," to pay this punishment on earth by doing penance, so that we do not come under God's judgment. Being disciplined in this way, "we may not be condemned along with the world" (1 Corinthians 11:31–32).

Since apostolic times, Christians have acknowledged that even after a sin has been forgiven by God, punishment for that sin may still remain (see 2 Samuel 12:13-14; CCC, 1473). One of the aims of penance is to make reparation for the punishment that remains (called "temporal punishment") after forgiveness.

Christians "have always endeavored to help one another on the path leading to the heavenly Father through prayer, the exchange of spiritual goods and penitential expiation"[10] (see Colossians 1:24). In this communion of saints, the earthly Church, which has the power to "bind…and loose" (Matthew 16:19), can extend the penances of Christ and the saints to take the place of our own temporal punishment: This is called an *indulgentia,* a favor. For centuries then, if a Christian said an "indulgenced" prayer, such as the Sign of the Cross, the prayer "loosened" the equivalent of, in this case, 150 days of fasting.

The Church revised the list of indulgences, contained in the *Manual of Indulgences*, in 1999. The English edition was published in 2006. The size of indulgences is no longer measured in terms of days and years of equivalent fasting. An indulgence is now either *partial*, taking away "some part" of that punishment, or *plenary*, taking away all of it. To be given a *plenary* indulgence, in addition to saying the given prayer, one also goes to the sacrament of penance in the same week, receives Holy Communion the same day and says a prayer for the intention of the Holy Father.

Most of the prayers that were once indulgenced in "days and years" are no longer indulgenced at all.[11] Our book numbers the remaining indulgences with the format "no. 4, s. 2" for example, to indicate indulgence grant number 4, section 2.

Indulgences, then, are *not* the remission of eternal punishment (hell); Christ's grace does that freely in the sacrament of penance. Indulgences are the remission of temporal punishment (purgatory).

and buried in the corners of properties. Blessed for obtaining "health of mind and body," the medal has been used as consolation for the sick and dying in the Blessing of Saint Maurus for the sick.

THE BROWN SCAPULAR

A scapular is actually a piece of monastic clothing, worn by Benedictines, Dominicans and Carmelites, among others. The *brown* scapular is part of the Carmelite habit: Its full version stretches from the neck to the feet.

In the Middle Ages laity began to relate closely with communities of friars and monks, often becoming associates of orders by placing themselves under their spiritual direction and joining what are called their "third orders." These lay members began to wear modified versions of the scapular, which shrank over time to the two-inch square that is the brown scapular today. A simple enrollment in the brown scapular associates one with the family of Mount Carmel but is not the same as becoming a member of the Carmelite third order.

Why would one wear this modified monastic habit? The Carmelite order is one of the most intensely Marian orders: the Carmelites say that Mary herself gave the original scapular to their superior general, Saint Simon Stock. The scapular is thus a sign of filial love and trust in Mary, the Mother of God—a mother who clothes her children.

Mary's reputed promise to Simon is on most scapulars: "Take this scapular: it shall be a sign of salvation, a protection in danger and a pledge of peace. Whoever dies wearing this garment shall not suffer eternal fire."

Mary promised the grace of an opportunity for final repentance to those who wear this habit and live the life it represents. A sign of devotion to Mary and trust in her assistance, the brown scapular recalls the Carmelites' unique commitment to prayer and symbolizes a monastic dedication to the virtues. The great John Paul II revealed, "I, too, have worn the Scapular of Carmel over my heart…out of love for our common heavenly Mother, whose protection I constantly experience."[12]

The apparition of Our Lady of Mount Carmel to Saint Simon Stock is commemorated on July 16. On this day you might ask a priest for enrollment in the brown scapular, found in the *Book of Blessings*.

Chapter Two

Days, Weeks, Months

S even Holy Tombs was mostly a Catholic neighborhood, but we always got Protestant weather," laments author John Powers in his fictionalized memoirs. In that era Catholic children stayed indoors on Good Friday out of respect for the passion and death of Christ. Powers, however, admits having spent "a lot of time between noon and three o'clock staring out the living room window at the non-Catholics," who were playing outdoors on that invariably bright and sunny afternoon.[1]

Even when the weather doesn't cooperate, Catholics have a sense of particularly sacred times—moments set aside for certain activities or dedicated to particular meditations. It is one of the ways the Church sanctifies the year.

HOURS OF THE DAY

"Seven times a day I praise you," sings the psalmist (Psalm 119:164). Jews and Christians have long aspired to lift their voices in prayer at certain times throughout the day; early monastics even attempted to say all 150 psalms every day. This practice gave birth to the Liturgy of the Hours, in which all the psalms were said in a weekly cycle of seven daily "hours."

Eventually the Hours became mandatory for religious orders and clergy. Lay interest in the Hours led to the widespread recitation of the rosary, consisting of 150 Hail Marys symbolizing the number of psalms. With the reforms of the Second Vatican Council, the cycle of psalms recited in the Hours was stretched out over a month, one of the seven hours was dropped; but, for the first time, the laity were specifically invited to participate.

Other devotions have arisen to similarly fill our days with prayer.

THE SIGN OF THE CROSS

On meeting Sabitha's grandmother Dorothy, Andrew was struck by her use of the Sign of the Cross. Each time we left her apartment, each time we left a house, each time Andrew turned the keys in the ignition, she crossed herself. An act of praise to the Holy Trinity, of sorrow for sin to the crucified Lord, of gratitude that the cross has been applied to our individual soul, of petition for whatever it precedes, the Sign of the Cross is perhaps the most basic Christian prayer.

At the end of the second century, Tertullian explained: "At every forward step,…at every going in and out, when we put on our clothes and shoes,…when we sit at table,…in all the ordinary actions of daily life, we trace upon the forehead the sign."[2]

THE MORNING OFFERING

As an act of self-offering, the Sign of the Cross takes on special significance in the morning. Saint John Vianney often spoke of the importance of making a morning offering. "Jesus Christ," he explained, "by His sufferings and His death, has made all our actions meritorious, so that for the good Christian there is no motion of our hearts or of our bodies which will not be rewarded if we perform them for Him."[3]

What does he mean by *meritorious?* The world was created so that through it humanity might come to love and praise God; but once humanity alienated itself from God, the earthly world and ordinary life were deprived of this purpose. With Christ's redemption the ordinary world was redeemed: The world can once again support beings who love and praise their Creator.

A Protestant friend once explained, "I may have led a 'good' life in high school, but it didn't 'count' because I didn't do it for love of Jesus." And that is the Catholic teaching on merit, on actions that "count": To be redeemed is to love God, and by keeping his commandments we remain God's friends and work out our salvation (see John 15:14; Philippians 2:12). We love God when we work or study well for his sake, when we enjoy the company of our family for the love of God, when we lovingly entrust ourselves to him before we sleep.

"All you have to do," specified Saint John Vianney, "is to have in view the object of pleasing God in everything you do." We need only, each morning as we awake, think of God, make the Sign of the Cross and offer our day to him. "Oh, how we could merit Heaven every day, my dear brethren, by doing just our ordinary duties, but by doing them for God and the salvation of our souls!"[4]

Here's one of many versions of the Morning Offering:

O my God, I adore, I love you with all my heart. I thank you for having created me, having saved me by your grace, and having preserved me during the night. I offer you all my prayers, works, joys, and sufferings of this day: grant that they may all be according to Your will and for Your greater glory. + Amen.

THE ANGELUS

The Angelus is a celebration of the very heart of Christianity: the conviction that God has become man in the Person of Jesus Christ. The Hail Mary is natural to this prayer, of course, because the Hail Mary is formed from the verses spoken by the archangel Gabriel and Saint Elizabeth in the events surrounding the Incarnation (see Luke 1:28, 42). The very name *Angelus* comes from the prayer's opening word in Latin, meaning "angel."

The Angelus is said three times a day: at six in the morning, twelve noon and six in the evening. The prayer is an ideal way to call to mind the essence of Christianity throughout the day. It even includes some "Catholic aerobics": When it is said standing, all genuflect at the words "and the Word became Flesh." During the Easter Season the hymn *Regina Coeli* usually replaces the Angelus.

Leader: The angel of the Lord declared unto Mary.

All: And she conceived of the Holy Spirit. Hail Mary, . . .

Leader: Behold the handmaid of the Lord.

All: Be it done unto me according to your word. Hail Mary,…

Leader: And the Word was made flesh.

All: And dwelt among us. Hail Mary,…

Leader: Pray for us, O holy Mother of God.

All: That we may be made worthy of the promises of Christ.

Leader: Let us pray.

All: Pour forth, we beseech you, O Lord, your grace into our hearts, that as we have known the incarnation of Christ, your Son, by the message of an angel, so by his passion and cross we may be brought to the glory of his resurrection, through the same Christ our Lord. Amen.[5]

EVENING PRAYERS

Morning and evening are primary hours of prayer in the Christian tradition, as evidenced by Lauds and Vespers in the Liturgy of the Hours. The psalmist says, "Let my prayer be counted as incense before you, / and the lifting up of my hands as an evening sacrifice!" (Psalm 141:2).

After a long day most of us would rather collapse in front of the television than lift our arms in praise, but make every effort to gather your family for evening prayers: They could be called the minimum of family liturgy. Say a decade or five of the rosary, sing and pray in honor of the particular devotion of the month, celebrate special feasts or seasons with special prayers, present family concerns before the altar of God. You'll have as many choices as TV, with no fighting over the remote! As Father Patrick Peyton famously said, "The family that prays together stays together."

THE DAYS OF THE WEEK

Just as Christians have set aside certain hours of the day for particular prayers and concerns, the Church also has sanctified specific days of the week. While the Jews kept the Sabbath on Saturday, the early Church soon kept its holy day on Sunday. Other days received their dedications, making the week a gradual unfolding of the story of Christ.

Wednesday: The Betrayal of Christ

Since apostolic times Christians have dedicated Wednesday, Thursday and Friday to the remembrance of the passion and death of Christ. Wednesday marked Judas's betrayal, for that is when he contacted the temple priests (see Mark 14:1–2, 10–11). Jews at the time of Christ fasted on Mondays and Thursdays; the *Didache*, the first-century body of teaching on morality and prayer, exhorts Christians to fast on Wednesdays and Fridays.[6]

In the Western Church Wednesday is an informally penitential day: though the Church does not prescribe penance, a number of people keep the Wednesday fast. Because Saint Joseph often is remembered on this day, the fast is sometimes kept as a prayer for the sanctity of the family and individual family members.

Thursday: The Last Supper and the Blessed Sacrament

The night before he died, our Lord took bread, blessed it, broke it and gave it to his disciples as truly his Body and Blood. Thursday is a special remembrance of this great gift— a gift that, Pope John Paul II wrote, the Church has received not as one gift among many but as *"the gift par excellence*, for it is the gift of himself, of his person in his sacred humanity, as well as the gift of his saving work."[7]

Priests may offer special votive Masses in honor of the Eucharist on this day. Some parishes continue the tradition of celebrating a "holy hour" of eucharistic adoration on Thursday evenings. Even if your parish does not expose the

Eucharist for adoration, we recommend making a special attempt to visit Jesus in the Blessed Sacrament today.

FRIDAY: THE PASSION AND DEATH OF CHRIST

Just as each Sunday is a "little Easter" and day of feasting, each Friday is also a "little Good Friday" and shares in its penitential character. Canon Law calls for abstinence from all meat products on every Friday of the year. Following the Second Vatican Council, national bishops' conferences were allowed to determine that, in their countries, the faithful would abstain from some other food, or the bishops could mandate some other act of penance (Canons 1251 and 1253).

The American bishops lifted the obligation of abstaining from meat in 1966 without prescribing a specific alternative act of penance, allowing Americans to fulfill their weekly obligation by whatever act of prayer, fasting or almsgiving they choose. Inspired by the example of Andrew's grandparents, we usually abstain from meat in solidarity with the universal Church.

SATURDAY: THE BLESSED VIRGIN MARY

Since the ninth century the Church has honored Mary with special votive Masses on Saturday mornings.[8] This commemoration is said to be related to the remembrance of Christ's passion on Friday and resurrection on Sunday, for it was Mary who kept hope in her divine Son, unshaken in faith between his death and rising.

Notre Dame grads, however, know that Saturdays belong to Our Lady because the Irish take the field that day. As legendary coach Lou Holtz often said, "God doesn't care who wins the football game, but his mother does. And her name is Notre Dame." As students, Saturday morning solemn Mass in honor of the Blessed Virgin became one of our most intense moments of weekly prayer.

SUNDAY: THE RESURRECTION

The parents of the human family, the book of Genesis makes clear, were created out of the goodness of God, given a world that supplied all their needs and set aside for the company of God, who "walk[ed with them] in the garden in the cool of the day" (Genesis 3:8). When they betrayed their vocation to love and obey God alone, however, this life of resting in God came to an end. They were expelled from the garden and left to labor "all the days of your life" (Genesis 3:17).

The *Catechism* confirms that the purpose of human life is "to know him, to love him," and that to accomplish this once again, "God sent his Son as Redeemer and Savior" (*CCC*, 1). The Garden of Paradise, where humanity rested in peace with God, will once again be opened upon our entrance into eternal beatitude: No longer toiling slaves, we again will live fully our human vocation. Even now we enjoy "the first fruits of the Spirit" (Romans 8:23): Because of the redemption of Christ, we have a foretaste of that rest in God here on earth.

Sunday is the day consecrated to resting in God. The laws that regulate the life of the Church insist that the faithful abstain "from such work or business that would inhibit the worship to be given to God, the joy proper to the Lord's Day, or the due relaxation of mind and body,"[9] often interpreted as more than four hours' servile work (see Canon 1247). This rest is not simply a "day off," a day to catch up on errands or get ahead on work, but rather, as Maria von Trapp reminds us, a "unique chance to surrender…entirely to God."[10]

Yes, we're actually obligated to relax, enjoy our friends and family and worship a loving God for one-seventh of our life: Redemption is a great thing! The height of this opportunity is Sunday Mass, of course, which the Church also insists is fundamental to Christian identity and to a continuing relationship with Christ, an opportunity that must be taken (Canon 1247).

Maria von Trapp vividly describes the old Austrian practice of Sunday. Around five on Saturday afternoon, bells rang to announce the beginning of preparations for Sunday: the home cleaned, people washed, "Sunday best"—clothes worn only on Sunday—ironed, part of Sunday dinner prepared. After a leisurely dinner, the rosary was said, and the readings or Mass prayers might be read in advance.

In the morning people donned the "Sunday best" and walked to church, even if this took hours. A large Sunday meal came at noon, and afterward friends would meet, children play, people dance, adults make music.[11]

In other parts of Europe, a candle would be lit during the evening meal in front of an image of the Holy Trinity: Today, the principal day of Christian worship, is the "feast" of the Triune God. During the meal parents would ask their children to recount the sermon's message, with the father asking questions and the mother helping to supply the answers.[12]

How feasible these visions of Sunday are must be determined individually. They provide beautiful sketches of a day that the Church gives to family, friends, acts of mercy and, above all, God.

THE MONTHS OF THE YEAR

Entire months also have become associated with specific mysteries of the faith, usually determined by principal feast days that fall during them. Many of these dedications are rather recent in origin, others quite venerable. All, however, provide opportunity for more sustained reflection on a particular theme than a single passing day might afford.

JANUARY: THE HOLY NAME OF JESUS

January became associated with the Holy Name of Jesus because January 1 commemorates, among other things, the naming of the holy child. "God has highly exalted him," Saint Paul affirms, "and bestowed on him the name which is above every name, that at the name of Jesus every knee should bow" (Philippians 2:9–10). The Feast of the Holy Name is celebrated on January 3.

Devotion to the Holy Name became widespread in the 1400s with the preaching of Saint Bernardine of Siena. At each city this famous friar would renounce the prominent vice. In Bologna he preached so effectively against gambling that the people lit bonfires to burn their decks of cards. A devastated card manufacturer demanded to know how he would feed his family. The saint suggested he print cards honoring the Holy Name. Since then the faithful have carried cards of the Holy Name or placed them in prayer books. People carved Jesus' name in wood to hang over their beds and doors as a way to invoke his assistance.

One can honor the name of Jesus Christ in other ways as well: Obeying the second commandment comes to mind. If your grandparents grew up Catholic, it is likely that they referred to Jesus Christ by name only in prayer; they probably called him "our Lord" in casual conversation. A slight bow of the head would accompany use of Jesus' name. During this month reflect on how you use the name of Jesus, whether too infrequently in prayer or too casually otherwise.

January Prayer (*Raccolta*, 122)

O God, who appointed your only begotten Son to be the Savior of mankind and commanded His name to be called Jesus; mercifully grant that we may enjoy the vision of Him in heaven, whose holy Name we venerate on earth. Through the same Christ our Lord. Amen.[13]

Hymns

Latin classic, *"Iesu Dulcis Memoria"* (*Raccolta*, 90)
English suggestion, "At the Name of Jesus Every Knee Shall Bow"

FEBRUARY: THE HOLY FAMILY

As many mystics have noted, our Lord spent three years in public ministry and thirty years in family life. In the home at Nazareth, Christ remained obedient to Mary and Joseph (see Luke 2:51). With Joseph's death, Jesus earnestly worked to support the household, continuing to live with his mother until the beginning of his public ministry.

Though it might be funny to imagine the Blessed Virgin Mary asking Jesus Christ to take out the garbage, his decision to spend his human life in this way is a radical affirmation of ordinary family life and work. Can we imagine that, in his most trying moments, our Lord did not think back to the happiest moments of his life, the days at home in Nazareth?

February Prayer (*Raccolta*, 126)

> Jesus, sweetest Child, who did dwell in holiness in the holy house at Nazareth, in subjection to your parents, wearied by poverty and toil, and did increase in wisdom, age, and grace, have mercy on us.

Hymn

"Once in Royal David's City"

MARCH: SAINT JOSEPH

Though he was from the house of King David, Joseph of Nazareth was a poor man (see Matthew 1:1–16; Luke 2:24; Leviticus 12:8). A kind and holy man, he was a carpenter (Matthew 1:19; 13:55). These are the few facts we know about him, but family life and fatherhood are experiences close to us all, from which we can imagine the happiness of the Holy Family and the character of so great a father. Indeed, "if one may judge of the greatness of the Saints by the importance of the charges confided to them, Saint Joseph must indeed be marvelously great."[14]

March Prayer (*Raccolta*, 472)

> Remember, O most pure spouse of the Virgin Mary, Saint Joseph, my beloved patron, that never has it been heard that any one invoked your patronage and sought your aid without being comforted. Inspired by this confidence, I come to you and fervently commend myself to you. Ah, despise not my petition, dear foster father of our Redeemer, but accept it graciously. Amen.

Hymn

Latin classic, *"Te Ioseph Celebrant Agmina Caelitum"*
English suggestion, "By All Your Saints Still Striving"

April: The Blessed Sacrament

Things seemed rough at Notre Dame. Many people were complaining that certain events were inappropriate at a Catholic university; many more complained that Catholicism amounted to a list of prohibitions. In the middle of it all, how could we assert the truth that Christianity makes a great positive contribution to our lives—namely, the love of Jesus Christ? We organized the first eucharistic procession on campus in almost fifty years. This caught the attention not only of the campus but of diocesan newspapers across the country.

Indeed, the central vocation of the apostles—and of all Christians—is simply "to be with" Jesus (Mark 3:14). For this reason the Eucharist is central to our life. Not only does Christ continually abide in the souls of all who eat his flesh and drink his blood (see John 6:56), but also he is continually present for us in the physical eucharistic species.

Praying before his presence in the Blessed Sacrament "has played a role in the [Western] church's devotional life similar to that of icons in the Orthodox tradition," theologian Brian Daley reflects, "…as manifestations in visible form of God's transcendent glory, nourishing and transforming our humanity."[15] The eucharistic bread is our greatest "icon" of Christ's presence in the Church and in the world, an icon that really *is* what it symbolizes. There Christ is present not simply like warm feelings within but as a real Person, present in the world so that we can be with him.

This month celebrate and proclaim the presence of Christ in the Eucharist. Take some time to adore the real presence.

Perhaps you can begin planning a eucharistic procession for the Feast of Corpus Christi, which falls in May or June.

April Prayer (partial indulgence, no. 8, s. 2)

> My Jesus, I believe that you are in the Blessed Sacrament. I love you above all things, and I long for you in my soul. Since I cannot now receive you sacramentally, come at least spiritually into my heart. As though you have already come, I embrace you and unite myself entirely to you; never permit me to be separated from you.[16]

Hymn

Latin classic, *"Tantum Ergo"*
English suggestion, "At That First Eucharist"

MAY: OUR LADY

"Mary gardens" have been growing in popularity. These gardens are filled with plants named for the Blessed Virgin, which include most popular flowers. The names of some are obviously connected to Our Lady: marigold, for example, Madonna lily and rosemary. The names of many, though, were secularized following the Reformation: Our Lady's Gloves became foxgloves; Our Lady's Crown become cornflower; Mary's Heart became bleeding heart. Lists that translate these secularized names into their religious names are common, and some research online will open up worlds of floral piety.

We suggest you choose a mix of flowers that will provide blossoms throughout the year. White flowers symbolize Mary's joys, red, her sorrows, and gold, her glories.

A Mary garden is not complete without a statue of Mary, of course. Catholic faithful throughout the Midwest shelter her statue in old bathtubs, buried halfway to provide an upside-down U-shaped grotto. Then again, some traditions can be improved.

May Prayer (partial indulgence, no. 17, s. 3)

> We fly to your patronage, O holy Mother of God; despise not our petitions in our necessities, but deliver us always from all dangers, O glorious and blessed Virgin.[17]

Hymn

Latin classic, *"Regina Coeli"*
English suggestion, "Sing of Mary"

JUNE: THE SACRED HEART OF JESUS

"Devotion to the Sacred Heart of Jesus," a contemporary theologian notes, "has suffered cardiac arrest."[18]

Popular images of the Sacred Heart can seem "weird," juxtaposing Christ's sugar-sweet facial expressions and bloody, tortured heart. Yet behind whatever cultural barriers separate us from this devotion lies the central truth of the heart of Jesus: God loves us with a human heart and a human love, with a love that extends through pain and death, "even death on a cross," to offer us redemption (Philippians 2:8; see John 3:16).

To spread awareness of his love for all people, Christ revealed the pains of his heart to Sister Margaret Mary Alacoque, seeking to counter Jansenists and Calvinists who taught otherwise. He asked that souls who loved him might console him in return. From these visions arose the popularity of receiving Holy Communion in reparation on the first Friday of each month. The Church grants a plenary indulgence (no. 3) for reciting the *Iesu Dulcissime*, a prayer of reparation, on the Feast of the Sacred Heart, nineteen days after Pentecost.

June Prayer (*Raccolta*, 263)

> O most holy Heart of Jesus, fountain of every blessing, I adore you, I love you, and with a lively sorrow for my sins, I offer you this poor heart of mine. Make me humble, patient, pure, and wholly obedient to your will. Grant, good Jesus, that I may live in you and for you. Protect me in the midst of danger; comfort me in my afflictions; give me health of body, assistance in my temporal needs, your blessing on all that I do, and the grace of a holy death.

Hymn

Latin classic, *"Cor, Acra Legem Continens"*
English suggestion, "To Jesus Christ Our Sovereign King"

JULY: THE PRECIOUS BLOOD

July had a bit of an identity crisis when the feast that gave this month its devotional theme, the Feast of the Precious Blood, was suppressed in the 1969 calendar revisions. However, speaking to pilgrims in July 2006, Pope Benedict recalled that July is "a month in which we traditionally venerate the Most Precious Blood of Christ." He asked pilgrims "to pray that modern humanity may experience the power of the Blood of Christ, poured out on the cross for our salvation,"[19] a request we recommend in perpetuity.

July Prayer (*Raccolta*, 221)

> Lord Jesus Christ, who came down from heaven to earth from the bosom of the Father, and shed your Precious Blood for the remission of our sins: we humbly beseech you, that in the day of judgment we may deserve to hear, standing at your right

hand: "Come, ye blessed." Who lives and reigns for ever and ever. Amen.

Hymn

Latin classic, *"Pange Lingua"*

English suggestion, "At the Lamb's High Feast We Sing"

AUGUST: THE IMMACULATE HEART OF MARY

Once again Mary is presented as the model Christian. As always, her perfections do not distance her from other Christians so much as they embody what each Christian is called, by the grace of God, to become.

In speaking of the Immaculate Heart, we must understand the biblical concept of *heart*, "the centre of human life, the point where reason, will, temperament and sensitivity converge, where the person finds his unity and his interior orientation."[20] The pure, the clean, the immaculate heart therefore describes the ideal believer, perfected in faith, morality, prayerful reflection and earthly detachment. It is freed from any of the separation from God that is sin. Such pure hearts "see God" (Matthew 5:8).

As the work of God perfected by grace, Mary becomes the model for all to imitate; indeed, we must never fear to set up model Christians for the imitation of all (see 1 Corinthians 4:16; Philippians 3:17; 1 Thessalonians 1:6; 2 Thessalonians 3:7, 9). In the Immaculate Heart we find the perfect response to the burning love of Christ's Sacred Heart.

August Prayer (*Raccolta*, 392)

Immaculate Virgin, who being conceived without sin, directed every movement of your most pure heart toward God, and was always submissive to his divine will; obtain for me the grace to hate sin with all my heart and to learn from you to live in perfect resignation to the will of God.

Hymn

Latin classic, *"O Sanctissima"*

English suggestion, "Immaculate Mary"

September: Our Lady of Sorrows

The Feast of Our Lady of Sorrows falls on September 15, but the whole month of September is dedicated to her sorrows. By custom the sorrows are seven in number: Simeon's foreboding prophecy (see Luke 2:34–35), the Holy Family's flight into Egypt (Matthew 2:13–14), losing Jesus in the temple (Luke 2:43–45), meeting Jesus on his way to Calvary, his crucifixion and death (John 19:25), his removal from the cross, and his burial (Mark 15:46; Luke 23:50–53). If Our Lady is often portrayed with surreal happiness, the reality of her life was nonetheless a true spiritual martyrdom.

Yet the life of faith is more than sorrow. We recall the great joy Christ the Savior brought to Mary, which she concretely experienced in seven particularly powerful moments: the Annunciation (Luke 1:26–38), her visit with Elizabeth (Luke 1:39–56), the Nativity (Luke 2:7), the adoration of the Magi (Matthew 2:11), the finding of our Lord in the temple (Luke 2:46), his resurrection (John 20), and Mary's own coronation in heaven (Revelation 12:1).

September Prayer (*Raccolta*, 385)

Most Holy Virgin and Mother, whose soul was pierced by a sword of sorrow in the passion of your divine Son, and who in his glorious resurrection was filled with never-ending joy at his triumph; obtain for us who call upon you, so to be partakers in the adversities of Holy Church and the sorrows of the sovereign pontiff, as to be found worthy to rejoice with them in the consolations for which we pray, in the charity and peace of the same Christ our Lord. Amen.

Hymn

Latin classic, *"Stabat Mater Dolorosa"*
English suggestion, "At the Cross Her Station Keeping"

OCTOBER: THE HOLY ROSARY

Ah, the rosary. Truly "old school" Catholics were able to say an entire Hail Mary in a single breath as they spun the beads through their fingers. More than a holy breathing exercise, though, the rosary is truly a compendium of the gospel. Though "clearly Marian in character," it is "at heart a Christocentric prayer."[21]

The rosary is an excellent example of a fundamental insight of Catholic spirituality, an insight that underlies many devotions described in this book: In order to seek the face of God, we must gaze upon the human face of Christ, for *Jesus Christ* is the Way to God (see John 14:6, 9). So we must approach God through the events of Christ's human life. In the rosary we contemplate Christ's joyful entrance into the world, his sorrowful passing from the world and glorious return; John Paul II added the luminous mysteries in his 2002 apostolic letter on the rosary, so now we also meditate on Christ's teaching and ministry.

The many Hail Marys of the rosary are very appropriate in this contemplation, for "the contemplation of Christ has an *incomparable model* in Mary."[22] It was Mary who, as the events of Christ's life unfolded, "kept all these things, pondering them in her heart" (Luke 2:19). John Paul II exhorted us, then, to pray the rosary with a quiet rhythm, a lingering pace and above all attention to the individual events it commemorates.

October Prayer (*Raccolta*, 402)

> O Virgin and Queen of the Holy Rosary, you are the Daughter of our heavenly Father, the Mother of God the Son, and the Bride of the Spirit with his sevenfold gifts. You can obtain all things from the ever-blessed Trinity, you must therefore obtain for me this favor which is so necessary for me, provided that it be no obstacle to my eternal salvation.

Hymn

Latin classic, *"Salve Regina"*

English suggestion, "Hail Holy Queen"

NOVEMBER: THE POOR SOULS

November is about one thing: those we love, burning in the fiery pit of purgatory. (Wait! Keep reading.)

A story from the nineteenth century tells of an Englishman being raised from the dead. Having seen purgatory, he was "a soul struck with fear of the judgments of God."[23] He had seen a deep valley, fire on one side, ice on the other, filled with innumerable souls; these poor souls fled to the warmth of the fire from the frigid ice, only to extinguish themselves in the ice when the heat became overwhelming. The perennial Christian response, appropriately, has always been, "Get them out of there!" This month, for the purification of these suffering yet holy souls, alms will be given, prayers and Masses will be offered, and fasting will be done.

OK, we have to square with you. We once heard some non-Catholics complaining about what the *Catechism of the*

Catholic Church says about the fires of purgatory. That was interesting, because the *Catechism* says nothing about them. Church teaching about purgatory is actually quite sparse, literally 0.104 percent of the *Catechism*. The Church affirms that Christian souls who die "in God's...friendship, but still imperfectly purified," undergo a purification (*CCC*, 1030).

Purgation is necessary because one cannot enter heaven, the full possession of God, with a heart still attached to things contrary to God (see *CCC*, 1030). This postmortem purification is entirely the grace and work of God, so we on earth can pray that this grace may be given to those who need it—just as we pray that any other grace may be granted to those in need. This is the Church's teaching on purgatory. The rest—the punishments, the location, the duration—is the result of the admirable medieval imagination, clothes that dress up the skeletal *doctrine* about purgatory quite nicely.

At the time of Christ, Jews who believed in the afterlife acknowledged that, upon death, "the soul goes either to an intermediate locale"—*sheol* or "the bosom of Abraham"—or "directly to eternal punishment in Gehenna or eternal reward in Eden" (see Luke 16:22-23).[24] Both the Old and New Testaments speak of Jewish practices of prayer for the dead (see 2 Maccabees 12:45; 1 Corinthians 15:29).

Writing between AD 197 and 206, Christian theologian Tertullian reiterated belief in the "bosom of Abraham," a place "though not in heaven,...yet higher than hell," where faithful souls await entrance into the full and everlasting happiness of Paradise.[25] Showing that the early Christians were no good at being Protestant, he continues, "As often as the anniversary comes round, we make offerings for the dead [on the anniversary of their death].... If, for these and other such rules, you insist on having positive Scripture injunction, you will find none. Tradition will be held forth to you as the originator of them, custom as their strengthener, and faith as their observer."[26]

In her autobiography Saint Perpetua recounts seeing her younger brother released to heaven on account of her prayers before her martyrdom in AD 203. Join in the Church's concern for her brothers and sisters, and pray for your dearly departed.

November Prayer (partial indulgence for souls in purgatory, no. 29, s.2)

> Eternal rest grant unto them, O Lord, and let perpetual light shine upon them. May they rest in peace.

Hymn

Latin classic, *"Dies Irae"*

English suggestion, "Day of Wrath, Day of Ire"

DECEMBER: THE DIVINE INFANT

Obviously, the devotion on everyone's mind this month is the divine infant. Your observance of Advent and Christmas should keep this theme before you! See chapter four for ideas on how to make this a Christ-centered season.

December Prayer

See chapter four.

Hymn

Latin classic, *"Alma Redemptoris Mater"*

English suggestion, Christmas carols!

Chapter Three

Milestones

abitha's family never does anything by halves. When her aunt acquired tickets for midnight Mass with the Holy Father, seventeen of them hopped a plane to Rome for Christmas. They explored the Eternal City, visited the grand churches of Christendom, received Pope John Paul II's apostolic blessing and celebrated the birth of our Lord in St. Peter's basilica—followed by their own enthusiastic celebration. Later, when Sabitha studied in Rome for a year, she witnessed the full spectrum of the Church's sacramental life played out in that great basilica: baptisms and confirmations at the Easter Vigil, first communicants on pilgrimage, newlyweds receiving the pope's special blessing at papal audiences, even the fulfillment of a life of faith in the beatifications and canonizations of blesseds and saints.

All were milestones on the earthly journey toward Christ, moments of renewed dedication that Christians have always marked with joy. Celebrating with friends, family, food and drink is a gospel truth (see John 2:1–11).

BAPTISM

Not unlike the book of Genesis, the Christian life begins with a watery chaos. Infants scream, cameras flash, godparents rush in after being held up in traffic—all while the new Christians' patron saints look on from heaven in, well, awe.

Truly a Christian does not begin this new life alone. The Church marks the new birth by asking that the child be given a Christian name, and, between the great legacy of biblical figures and later saints, there are plenty of role models from which to choose. Godparents commit to guiding the newly baptized to an adult relationship with Christ. This bond often forms an important part of the fabric in Mexican communities. A child can ask anything of his or her *compadres*. Their "house is his, [their] belongings are at his disposition."[1] For the rest of us, maintaining connection between sponsor and catechumen can be done in simple ways, like exchanging letters on the anniversary of baptism.

Saint Paul describes baptism as "put[ting] on Christ" (Galatians 3:27). For this reason the Church clothes the newly baptized in robes of white (see Revelation 7:9). In some places these robes are handmade and passed down in the family. A new cap is made for baby girls by folding a nice handkerchief into quarters, then sewing the three bottom layers together. The bottom point of the top layer can be tucked back and tacked in place if desired. After the baptism all stitches are removed, and the handkerchief is carried later as the "something old" at the girl's wedding.

The Church also presents to the newly baptized a candle, symbolizing Christ, "the light [who] shines in the darkness" (John 1:5). Keep it safe, and bring it out every year on the anniversary of the baptism. The Church so earnestly recommends renewal of baptismal promises on that anniversary that it grants a plenary indulgence for it (no. 28, s. 1). This event might be a celebration in itself, with promises renewed in front of the family altar, candle burning and a nice meal afterward.

PATRON FEAST

The feast day of a person's patron saint, one's "name day," is celebrated more enthusiastically than birthdays in some Catholic countries. In America the scale of name-day celebrations will probably be smaller, but that allows for a more spiritually focused celebration and a few religious gifts. Medals, holy cards or a book such as a saint's biography would be thoughtful presents.

Name days present a twofold opportunity: to learn and celebrate the life of the saint as well as to encourage a person to grow in sanctity, becoming more like the patron. No name day should begin without a morning serenade of *Las Mañanitas*; the lyrics and music are perhaps available from a Spanish teacher near you or, alternatively, online.

A simple way to mark one's patron feast day is with a dessert celebration with family and friends. Some saints even have a dessert associated with them: Madeleine cookies are named after Saint Mary Magdalene.

Arrange the table to include an image of the saint, flowers and perhaps a vigil candle. Begin the celebration with a prayer for the saint's intercession, and enjoy an evening that reinforces a culture of faith. To emphasize that our Lord is truly a part of your household of faith, celebrate the name days of both him and his mother—January 3 and September 12, respectively.

FIRST COMMUNION

When a nest of pelicans faces the danger of starvation, the mother will pierce her own breast so that her young might survive on her life-giving blood.[2] Although this isn't exactly true, the early Christians thought that it was, and the pelican became a powerful symbol of the Eucharist.

Celebrating First Communion is a special occasion in the childhood of any Catholic. In our families a huge feast complements the eucharistic meal, and gifts abound. The presence of family makes the event more meaningful: for Andrew, "important occasion" was defined by the presence of Grandma Mary and Grandpa John; Sabitha's First Communion, celebrated with her brother's baptism, was a family reunion of cross-country magnitude.

All this excitement is a wonderful way to highlight the importance of First Communion in the mind of a child, for the Eucharist is the "source and summit of the Christian life."[3] To emphasize the fact that First Communion is primarily about further initiating the child's relationship with Christ, take the opportunity to give gifts that foster a life of prayer: a rosary, brown scapular and missal are traditional, though a nice medal, Bible or crucifix will be treasured.

MARRIAGE

In the early Middle Ages, high dowries could prevent the celebration of marriage until late in life. To allow poor couples to begin families while they were able, the Church allowed them to begin their "married life" after the simpler celebration of the Rite of Solemn Engagement.

This is no longer the case: Unlike those medievals, you

don't get out of planning a wedding, as exhausting as that can be. But exactly because those preparations are so time-consuming, couples today must be careful not to forget to prepare for the sacrament of matrimony itself. The period before marriage should be a time of prayer and spiritual growth.

The Church still offers the Order for the Blessing of an Engaged Couple, which could be the "special occasion" of prayer you're looking for. The rite is a low-key celebration with family and can be found in *Catholic Household Blessings & Prayers*.[4] The formal rite is in the *Book of Blessings.*

Many marriage customs revolve around the fact that the sacrament is a symbol of Christ's relationship with the Church. The bride's white wedding attire, for example, recalls that Christ the Bridegroom is preparing the Church to be his bride, "holy and without blemish" (Ephesians 5:26–27). The veil is a symbol of the bride's modesty and virginity.[5]

Polish brides wear a wreath of flowers and herbs with their veil, which afterward is saved in the hope chest. When virginity gives way to motherhood, the dried wreath is crumbled in the baby's bath, emphasizing the bond between marriage and family.[6]

Many couples today honor the *sancta et immaculata* Blessed Virgin, icon of the entire Church, by presenting her with a bouquet of flowers after Communion as a means of seeking her intercession in their married life.

In the lives of Isaac and Jacob we glimpse the biblical legacy of parental blessing, which the Poles continue in the marriage ceremony. Originally the groom would ask for his parents' blessing before leaving their home and then go on to ask the bride's parents for their blessing. More recently the custom has moved to the church, where both sets of parents extend their blessing during the ceremony.

The ritual is simple and adaptable: Set up a small table with a crucifix, a candle, a bowl of holy water and a bundle of herbs, which the Polish call *kropidlo*. The couple kneel and thank their parents for giving them life, then ask the parents for their blessing. Each parent—first the groom's mother, then the groom's father, the bride's mother and ending with the bride's father—responds with a blessing and prayer for fidelity and love. At the end of the bride's father's blessing, all say three Our Fathers for the repose of the souls of departed family members.[7]

Scripture contains many appropriate blessings, among them Moses' blessing of the Israelites: "The LORD bless you and keep you: / The LORD make his face to shine upon you, and be gracious to you: / The LORD lift up his countenance upon you, and give you peace" (Numbers 6:24–26).

Some Hispanics incorporate the *lazo*, or "lasso," into the wedding as a symbol of the central place of prayer in binding together family life. The *lazo* consists of a figure-eight band, often made of two large rosaries that share one crucifix. After the vows the *lazo* is placed around the shoulders of the kneeling bride and groom. It remains there until after Communion as a symbol of their shared life.[8]

Ah, but what to get the couple who have everything? German glass blowers in Bavaria have the answer. The Bride's Tree, which has been growing in popularity, is a set of twelve traditional glass Christmas ornaments that symbolize the aspirations of the new couple. We recommend avoiding prepackaged sets, which are overpriced.

SYMBOLISM OF THE BRIDE'S TREE

Heart: The importance of love in the newly formed home

House: Good family shelter

Flower basket: Abundant beauty in the home

Basket of fruit: A Christian spirit of selfless giving

Teapot: Hospitality

Bird in a nest: Confidence and happiness in the home

Pinecone: Eternity

Animal: Peace with nature

Fish: Christ (The Greek word for "fish," *ichtus*, abbreviates "Jesus Christ: God, Son, Savior.")

Rose: Mary, the *Rosa Mystica*, a title dating from the fifth century[9]

Church (or angel): The importance of a family's worship of God

Saint Nicholas: Generosity

HOLY ORDERS

Annual ordinations make for one of the most moving weekends at Notre Dame. Prostrate before the altar, the candidates give their lives to the service of Christ, then emerge to the peal of triumphant bells and the buzz of happy crowds.

During the ordination service the hands of the new priests, which will consecrate the Body of Christ, are anointed with sacred chrism. In many places, such as the Philippines, the faithful kiss these newly ordained hands in gratitude to God. One either kneels (on the left knee alone) or bows profoundly, kissing the palms of both hands.

Some priests find this to be very humbling and beautiful; others report being "creeped out." But kissing the hands of a priest is not uncommon. Swiss children were once taught to kiss the hands of any priest they met until the day of their First Communion. Eastern Catholics, in fact, kiss the hands of their priests each time they are blessed.

At an ordination don't ask for the priest's *first* blessing: that belongs to his parents. The Church considers a priest's first Mass so important that he and all who attend are granted a plenary indulgence (no. 27, s. 1).

PILGRIMAGE

A pilgrimage is a trip to a shrine, a sacred place consecrated to God. Extremely popular in the Middle Ages, pilgrimages were how people went out and saw the world. But they are more than simply Christocentric recreation. The Church describes pilgrimage as "journeying between the obscurity of the faith and the thirst for the vision of clarity, tribulation and the desire for everlasting life, the weariness of the journey and the rest awaiting, between exile and homeland, between frenetic activity and contemplation."[10] A pilgrimage is an act of faith, undertaken in a spirit of prayer and often penance. It is a physical journey symbolizing our journey toward God.

To underscore the spiritual nature of a pilgrimage, select a patron saint to guide you along the way.[11] Saint Christopher, Saint Raphael and the Magi come to mind. In Renaissance Italy, when a son took a long journey, parents would commission a painting of the archangel Raphael leading their son, depicted as Tobias (see Tobit 5:20–21).[12]

Of the Magi Pope Benedict XVI observed, "Like the Magi, all believers—and young people in particular—have been called to set out on the journey of life in search of truth, justice and love.... The ultimate goal of the journey can only be found through an encounter with Christ."[13]

The world is full of famous pilgrimage sites, such as the Holy Land, Lourdes and the Camino de Santiago in Spain. Rome, however, is the queen of pilgrimage destinations.

The pope joins all pilgrims assembled outside his window each Sunday for noon Angelus, except in August, when no one wants to be in Rome anyway. If you wish to attend his general audience on Wednesday morning, your parish priest or bishop can help you get tickets, or you can contact the North American Pontifical College in Rome. The Wednesday audience includes a special blessing for newlyweds, who usually wear their wedding attire; request a *sposi novelli* ticket to be included in this ceremony.

If you wish to see the first pope, Saint Peter's bones have been unearthed in a Roman burial ground beneath the altar of St. Peter's basilica. This area is known as the *Scavi*. Reserve tickets in advance through the Vatican Web site.

The *Scala Sancta*, or Holy Stairs, must be the largest relic in Rome. Saint Helen brought to Rome these stairs of Pontius Pilate's mansion, which Christ ascended during his Passion (see Matthew 27:27). Today pilgrims ascend these steps on their knees, reciting particular prayers that can be found at the bottom of the stairs.

Helen also brought back the cross of Christ, much of which can be venerated at the Church of Santa Cruce. That church is part of the pilgrim's power walk, a seven-church tour promoted by Saint Philip Neri, which also includes St. Lawrence Outside the Walls, St. Sebastian's and the four patriarchal basilicas: St. Mary Major, St. Paul Outside the Walls, St. John Lateran and of course St. Peter's.

If you want a more relaxed pace, the Church grants a plenary indulgence for visiting any one of the four patriarchal basilicas and there reciting the Our Father and Creed (no. 33, s. 1). However you structure your trip, prayer is the center of each church visit. We recommend praying a decade of the rosary before the Blessed Sacrament at each stop.

DEATH AND DYING

Catholics have always taken death seriously, praying frequently for that hour when we will stand in judgment before the Lord. We have a special patron in this preparation: Saint Joseph. Because Scripture suggests that he died before the beginning of Christ's public ministry, he fulfilled the hope of all Christians—dying in the arms of Jesus and Mary, his family.

When Sabitha was little, her grandmother Dorothy taught her a daily prayer for a happy death: "Jesus, Mary and Joseph, I give you my heart and my soul. Jesus, Mary and Joseph, may I breathe forth my soul in peace with you. Amen."

A SHRINE NEAR YOU

Almost certainly you can find a shrine within a day's journey of wherever you are. Here are a few; the Internet, of course, can suggest many more.

- Holy Hill (National Shrine of Mary, Help of Christians): Hubertus, Wisconsin

- National Shrine of the Immaculate Conception: Washington, D.C.

- Marytown (National Shrine of Saint Maximilian Kolbe): Chicago, Illinois

- North American Martyrs: Auriesville, New York

- Basilica of San Carlos Borromeo: Carmel, California

When the hour of death comes, the Church tries to offer as much solace in the grace and person of Jesus Christ as possible. The last rites include the sacraments of anointing of the sick, reconciliation and *viaticum* (Communion for the dying), as well as a plenary indulgence (no. 12). Many Catholics, like Andrew's grandparents, keep a "sick-call set" (a crucifix with a container of holy water, cotton and blessed candles) to furnish the priest who comes to administer the last rites in the home. In that case someone greets the priest at the door, carrying a lit candle to honor the presence of Christ in the Eucharist, which the priest brings.

Even if someone dies without the ministry of a priest, the Church grants a plenary indulgence, provided the person prayed somewhat regularly during life and, near the

THE RESTING PLACES OF THE TWELVE APOSTLES

- Saint Peter: underneath the high altar, St. Peter's Basilica, Rome

- Saint James the Greater: Church of St. James, Compostela, Spain

- Saint John: tomb at Ephesus, Turkey (relics dispersed)

- Saint Andrew: reliquary pier, St. Peter's Basilica, Rome

- Saint Philip and Saint James the Lesser: Church of the Twelve Apostles, Rome

- Saint Bartholomew: within the high altar, Church of St. Bartholomew, Rome

- Saint Matthew: Church of St. Matthew, Salerno, Italy

- Saint Thomas: Santhome Cathedral, Chennai, India, or Cathedral of Ortona, Italy

- Saint Jude: Altar of Saint Joseph, St. Peter's Basilica, Rome

- Saint Simon the Zealot: Altar of the Crucifixion, St. Peter's Basilica, Rome

- Saint Matthias: St. Mary Major, Rome

- Saint Paul: underneath the high altar, Church of St. Paul Outside the Walls, Rome moment of death, raises the heart to God, perhaps kissing a crucifix (no. 12, ss. 2, 3).

The Church offers many ways of remembering our beloved dead. There is prayer at the vigil or wake the evening before the funeral, particularly the rosary. At burial in many Christian countries, mourners sprinkle holy water into the grave, sanctifying the ground where the body will rise to meet its Lord.

The Salzmanns continue the tradition of Gregorian Masses, a series of thirty consecutive Masses for the deceased. Pope Gregory the Great inspired this practice. After offering thirty Masses for the repose of a friend's soul, the pope saw the friend enter eternal beatitude.

The Church also grants a partial indulgence to souls at whose graves we pray (no. 29, s. 2). Andrew vividly remembers visits to his Uncle Terry's grave, the family kneeling as they prayed the Our Father, Hail Mary, Glory Be and "Eternal rest grant unto him,…".

Chapter Four

Advent and Christmas

At Notre Dame our friends dismissed us as "Nativitists." They invented this smear to designate the "heresy" of believing that Christmas is more important than Easter.

Granted, most mainstream theologians (including the *Catechism of the Catholic Church*, 1169) will tell you that Easter is the "feast of feasts," the center of the liturgical year. But for true Christmas devotees, the question is not so clearly settled. Consider it a Catholic version of the old question "Which came first, the chicken or the egg?" Sure, Jesus came to lay down his life for the salvation of the world, but could he have died and risen if he hadn't been born in the first place?

MAKE WAY FOR THE LORD

Advent is the time of preparation before Christmas—or rather, the time of preparation before the celebration of the Incarnation of God. Christmas, the coming of the Messiah, is the event for which the entire Jewish world sighed and prayed. For four short weeks we Christians recall their anxious waiting. In the readings at Mass, we express our own longing for the return of the Messiah and seek to prepare ourselves for that final coming.

But *how* to prepare? There are different approaches to

Advent, as you may know. Some people believe it is a time of joyful "anticipation." Others hold the philosophy, "As long as the priest's wearing violet, I'm doing penance."

This Advent dichotomy has a longer history than one might expect. In the fourth century the Church in Gaul promoted fasting and penance throughout the weeks prior to Christmas, while in the seventh century, the Church at Rome emphasized prayers that reflected a spirit of joyful expectation. By the twelfth century the practices of both the Roman and Gallican Churches had more or less fused, giving rise to a season of both sincere penance, which prepared and purified the soul for the coming of the Redeemer, and joyful prayer, awaiting the Hope of Ages soon to be born. The 1918 revision of the Code of Canon Law lifted the *obligation* to do penance during Advent, but for what it's worth, a true Nativitist will fast like there's no tomorrow—or at least like there's no Lent around the corner.

PREPARING THE MANGER

One custom blends hopeful prayer and worldly penance quite well. At the beginning of Advent, set up a rather large crib in your prayer corner. Next obtain a fair amount of straw, probably at ridiculously inflated prices from the local craft store. Throughout the day, whenever someone in the home offers some silent self-sacrifice—whether it be the traditional acts of prayer, fasting and almsgiving or a more humble sacrifice, such as letting someone else choose what to have for dinner—that person can add a piece of straw to the crib. In this way small acts of kindness and sacrifice prepare a welcoming home for the baby Jesus.

When you place the child Jesus in the manger, you can also decorate the manger with Saint Lucy's Wheat and Saint Barbara's Twig (see chapter seven). These symbolize how the merits of the saints beautify and accompany the suffrages we offer.

ADVENT PRAYERS, WREATHS AND CALENDARS

Each night the family gathers around the crib for a moment of prayer. You might begin with the opening prayer from the day's Mass, then light the Advent wreath, perhaps topping the night off with a decade or five of the rosary.

The use of Advent wreaths varies from house to house. You might light it every day of the week during your nightly prayer service or only on Sundays during the evening meal, using an Advent calendar during the nightly prayer services instead.

Metal Advent wreath frames can be purchased at Catholic bookstores or on the Internet. You can add pine branches, which are easy to obtain: your local Christmas tree seller probably has tons of branches strewn across his lot.

The three purple candles of the wreath symbolize the spirit of penance that marks this season. The single rose candle reflects the rose vestments worn on the Third Sunday of Advent. *Never* mistake the liturgical color rose for "pink": priests get very particular about this. Rose symbolizes joy; it is used because the *introit* for the Mass of this Sunday begins with the word *gaudete* or "rejoice." It is a reminder that, even in the midst of penitential seasons, Christians have reason to hope and rejoice: The Savior is coming.

CHRISTKINDL

To add a personal dimension to your Advent preparations, you might consider the Austrian custom of *Christkindl*. The names of participants are written on paper, and everyone picks a name from a hat. Each participant prays daily for the chosen person, sending small gifts such as holy cards, candy and notes of a prayer said for them that day. The goal is to go undiscovered until Christmas Day: It's the holy version of "Secret Santa."[1]

ADVENT PRAYER

Andrew first encountered this classic Advent prayer in a box of his great-grandmother's holy cards. The prayer is fairly popular. It is customarily said fifteen times throughout the day, beginning with the Feast of Saint Andrew on November 30.

> Hail and blessed be the hour and moment in which the Son of God was born of the most pure Virgin Mary, at midnight, in Bethlehem, in piercing cold. In that hour vouchsafe, O my God, to hear my prayer and grant my desires, through the merits of our Savior Jesus Christ, and of his blessed Mother. Amen.

THE CHRISTMAS NOVENA (DECEMBER 16)

The Christmas novena consists of the nine days immediately prior to Christmas, days marked by more intense preparation. The Christmas novena was especially important to Hispanic and Germanic cultures; in her famous book *Death Comes for the Archbishop*, Willa Cather's missionaries judge their success in part by the fervor with which the native converts keep the novena. The Church continues to encourage the faithful to keep the novena, granting a partial indulgence to those who attend a public novena (no. 22, s. 1). Here are some suggestions for your novena.

HERBERGSUCHEN OR *LAS POSADAS*

The *herbergsuchen* ("shelter seeking") reenacts Mary and Joseph's increasingly desperate search for shelter in the days leading up to the birth of the Christ child. You will need to obtain a picture of Saint Joseph leading the Blessed Virgin as they sought shelter, or you might use the figures of Mary and Joseph from your nativity set. Each day of the Christmas novena, these images are moved from one room to another. Each night the two are hosted by a member of the household, who through hospitality and friendly prayer attempts to "make up" for the hardships endured by the Holy Family at the hands of indifferent strangers during those days.

Maria von Trapp explained the Austrian custom of decorating a little altar in each room with candles and fir branches; the host would then spend as much time with the Holy Family as possible—perhaps even joining them for meals and always filling the time with conversational prayer.[2] At night, before evening prayers, the household would congregate outside the room that hosted the Holy Family and then carry them in solemn procession to their next host, singing Advent songs all the way. Next came night prayers, including the novena prayers.

The *herbergsuchen* works best when all the participants live under the same roof. If you can coordinate several residences, consider the similar Mexican custom of *Las Posadas*, which Sabitha experienced growing up in Texas. Spanish for "the inns," *Las Posadas* is also a re-creation of Mary and Joseph's search for a place to stay in Bethlehem. Two individuals play Mary and Joseph, and the rest of the group follow as they journey from residence to residence, rebuffed by the "innkeeper" at each one.

Traditionally this journey is spread over nine nights starting December 16, though *Las Posadas* celebrations at Notre Dame have been condensed into a single, much more manageable night. Singing traditional songs, a procession following Mary and Joseph were turned away from each dormitory they visited. The evening ended with Mexican hot chocolate and *churros*—and prayer.

HERBERGSUCHEN SONG

Adapted from Wer Klopfet An, *to the tune of "Are You Sleeping?"*

Who is knocking, who is knocking, at my door, at
my door?
> Two so poor and lowly, two so poor and lowly,
> at your door, at your door.

What can I do, what can I do, in this cold, in this cold?
> Grant a bit of shelter, grant a bit of shelter, from this
> cold, from this cold.

Just some rest, sir, just some rest, sir, for my wife, for
my wife.
> No more room today, sir, no more room today, sir,
> for your wife, for your wife.

THE "O ANTIPHONS"

You will find that there are scant few Advent hymns circulating in English. By far the most popular is "O Come, O Come, Emmanuel," which many people mistake for a Christmas carol. In fact it is an English popularization of the classical antiphons sung at Vespers during the week before Christmas. Each antiphon is drawn from the book of Isaiah, interpreted as a prophecy of the coming Savior. You might sing the appropriate verse each day before Christmas, as Mary and Joseph continue their search for shelter.

December 17: *O Sapientia.* "O come, thou Wisdom,…" (Isaiah 11:2–3; 28:29; 1 Corinthians 1:30)

December 18: *O Adonai.* "O come, O come, thou Lord of might,…" (Isaiah 11:4; 33:22; *CCC,* 209)

December 19: *O Radix Jesse.* "O come, thou Rod of Jesse,…" (Isaiah 11:1, 10)

December 20: *O Clavis David.* "O come, thou Key of David,…" (Isaiah 9:7; 22:22)

December 21: *O Oriens.* "O come, thou Dayspring,…" (Isaiah 9:1–2; Malachi 4:2; Luke 1:78)

December 22: *O Rex Gentium.* "O come, Desire of Nations,…" (Isaiah 2:4)

December 23: *O Emmanuel.* "O come, O come, Emmanuel,…" (Isaiah 7:14; 8:8)

PRAYERS FOR THE CHRISTMAS NOVENA (*RACCOLTA,* 125)

Leader: Eternal Father, I offer to your honor and glory, for my eternal salvation and for the salvation of the whole world, the mystery of the birth of our divine Redeemer.

All: Glory be to the Father, and to the Son, and to the Holy Spirit, as it was in the beginning, is now, and ever shall be, world without end. Amen.

Leader: Eternal Father, I offer to your honor and glory, for my eternal salvation and for the salvation of the whole world, the sufferings of the most holy Virgin and Saint Joseph on that long and weary journey from Nazareth to Bethlehem, and the anguish of their hearts at not finding a place of shelter when the Savior of the world was about to be born.

All: Glory be to the Father…

Leader: Eternal Father, I offer to your honor and glory, for my eternal salvation and for the salvation of the whole world, the sufferings of Jesus in the manger where he was born, the cold he suffered, the tears he shed, and his tender infant cries.

All: Glory be to the Father…

Leader: Eternal Father, I offer to your honor and glory, for my eternal salvation and for the salvation of the whole world, the humility, mortification, patience, charity, and all the virtues of the Child Jesus; I thank you, I love you, and I bless you infinitely for this ineffable mystery of the Incarnation of the Word of God.

All: Glory be to the Father…

Leader: The Word was made flesh;

All: And dwelt among us.

Leader: Let us pray. O God, whose only begotten Son has appeared in the substance of our flesh, grant, we beseech you, that through him, whom we acknowledge to be like us in his outward seeming, we may deserve to be renewed in our inward selves. Who lives and reigns with you for ever and ever. Amen.

CHRISTMAS EVE

As anyone who has grown up in Europe or read Laura Ingalls Wilder knows, the night of Christmas Eve is the traditional time to decorate the Christmas tree. You can add to a Paradise tree if you have one (see the Feast of Adam and Eve, chapter seven), or start fresh.

Your Christmas tree means a lot more than you might think. The custom is said to date back to Saint Boniface, the "Apostle to Germany," who cut down a sacred oak tree dedicated to the god Thor at Geismar. In replacement he offered the distraught Germans a fir tree as a symbol of Christianity.

The saint is supposed to have explained the symbolism of the tree: The fir is a humble tree, used to build homes; let Christ be at the center of the home. The fir leaves remain green in the darkest days; let Christ be your constant light. Its boughs reach out as if in an embrace and reach up as if to the heavens; let Christ be your comfort and your guide. In a sweeping gesture of ecumenism, we admit that Martin Luther is said to be the first who cut these trees down and brought them inside.

The ornaments are also significant. Your Paradise tree already has two decorations, apples and cookies. The apples represent the Fall, the food of death that caused Adam and Eve's expulsion from the earthly Paradise (see Genesis 3:17–23). The cookies are symbols of redemption, representing the Blessed Eucharist, the Bread of Life consumed by Christians, which leads to our entry into the heavenly paradise (see John 6:51).

A red garland, or string of red berries, wrapped around the tree recalls the love Christ expressed in his Passion, which binds together all Christians. The star on the tree represents the star that led the Magi in their quest for the Christ child, just as all Christians seek the Lord. The lights on the tree celebrate Jesus Christ as the Light of the World (see John 9:5) and represent the flame of his love.

Consider adding some of these traditional Bavarian ornaments to your Christmas tree:

Acorns, symbols of death and rebirth, recall Christ's admonition, "Unless a grain of wheat falls into the earth and dies, it remains alone; but if it dies, it bears much fruit" (John 12:24). In this sense acorns predict the coming death and resurrection of the child born today. Technically, the Hebrew says "grain of wheat." Tell it to the Bavarians.

Angels announced the birth of Christ to the shepherds (see Luke 2:8–15).

Candy canes, invented in England in the seventeenth century as a homage to the Christ child, are shaped like the staff of the shepherds who came to adore the Good Shepherd. Three small stripes recall the Holy Trinity, and one broad stripe symbolizes the Passion of our Lord (see Isaiah 53:5).

Drums recall the legend of the little drummer boy, who came to adore the newborn child with his gift of a simple song on his drum. The story, the popular carol and the ornament remind us that gifts given from the heart are precious, no matter how humble.

Eagles in medieval times were believed to have the power of eternal youth. When they grew old, they would fly "up to the height of heaven," burning away the marks of old age. Then they would dive three times into a fountain far below, emerging "renewed with a great vigor of plumage and splendor of vision." It should be no surprise that medievals used eagles as a symbol of baptism.[3]

Lambs were offered by the Jewish priests every year at Passover as sin offerings. As the Gospel of John is careful to lay out, Jesus Christ, the Lamb of God, was also killed as a sin offering, not simply for the Jewish people and for that year but for all people of all times (see John 11:49–52). Jesus is the reason for the season, but even a Nativitist must admit that his death is the reason for the Incarnation.

For more suggestions see the list for the Bride's Tree, a wedding gift we recommended, on p. 53.

This is not to say that you shouldn't include on your tree the Hallmark mice dressed like crayons or the miniature space shuttle purchased during the last family trip. Andrew's dad carefully recounts the history of each such special ornament every year as it is put on (or taken off) the tree: when it was purchased, from where, what each recalls. This time of familial reflection can be a meaningful part of Christmas. Your Christ-centered ornaments can add to the mix, acknowledging Christ along with the family memories.

MIDNIGHT MASS

Christmas Day traditionally begins with midnight Mass, as this is the "official" coming of the Christ child. Here Jesus is born anew, early Christmas Day, on the altar of the Church and in the depths of faithful hearts. In fact, popular dedication to midnight Mass on Christmas Eve throughout the Catholic world is quite impressive.

If you are going to attempt this ascetical feat, we suggest

the Austrian custom of a family nap, beginning around 8:00 PM. Someone, traditionally the father of the family, needs to rouse the rest in time to leave for Mass. With lantern in hand he serenely awakens everyone, singing carols such as "Silent Night." As family members get up and dressed, they emerge from their rooms carrying their own lanterns and join the singing.[4] We're quite sure the Austrians of previous generations didn't process on carpet, which emits noxious chemical fumes if it catches fire.

Your procession might move to the Christmas crib you've been preparing with straw, or at least to your nativity scene. There you officially mark Christ's birth by placing the baby in his manger before the group proceeds to Mass.

A QUICK SERVICE TO MARK THE BIRTH OF CHRIST

The Proclamation of the Birth of Christ

Leader:

Today, the twenty-fifth day of December,

unknown ages from the time when God created the heavens and the earth

and then formed man and woman in his own image.

Several thousand years after the flood,

when God made the rainbow shine forth as a sign of the covenant.

Twenty-one centuries from the time of Abraham and Sarah;

thirteen centuries after Moses led the people of Israel out of Egypt;

Eleven hundred years from the time of Ruth and the Judges;

one thousand years from the anointing of David as King;

in the sixty-fifth week according to the prophecy of Daniel.

In the one hundred and ninety-fourth Olympiad;

in the seven-hundred and fifty-second year from the foundation of the city of Rome.

The forty-second year of the reign of Octavian Augustus;
the whole world being at peace,

*[The image of the child Jesus is held up reverently, for the group
to see.]*

Jesus Christ, eternal God and Son of the eternal Father,

desiring to sanctify the world by his most merciful coming,

being conceived by the Holy Spirit,

and nine months having passed since his conception,

[All kneel, as the child is placed in the manger.]

was born in Bethlehem of Judea of the Virgin Mary.

[Very solemnly]

Today is the nativity of our Lord Jesus Christ according to
the flesh.

All: Amen.[5]

THE CHRISTMAS FEAST

"This day is holy…. Eat the fat and drink sweet wine…and
do not be grieved, for the joy of the Lord is your strength"
(Nehemiah 8:9–12).

Because the Christmas feast is common to so many
Catholic cultures, it is difficult to generalize how it is celebrated, but we'll try anyway. The large Christmas meal is
usually served on Christmas Eve, not Christmas Day (except
among the Irish). It follows a long day of fasting, during
which only small, meatless meals are eaten; until 1983 Canon
Law mandated fasting and abstinence on this day. In fact, if
the meal is consumed before midnight Mass, traditionally it
does not include meat; but most cultures have preferred to
eat the meal after Mass.

The Poles put a thin layer of straw under the white table-cloth, to recall the poverty of the God-child born in a stable, and set an extra place for this guest at their table.[6] Serbian Christians each bring a lit candle to the table, which the father of the family then places in one dish, symbolizing the union of the family.[7]

The meal begins with prayer. The head of the family says a special grace; if your family fears spontaneous prayer, use the "official" Christmas prayer that follows. Those not averse to the extemporaneous include a special invocation of God's blessing upon the family for health, success, peace and good will. A prayer is said for the holy souls, especially for those of the family—and especially for any who died during the previous year.

The meal itself is often highly ritualized. Italians tend to serve thirteen dishes, to represent the attendance at the Last Supper. The Poles serve seven, nine or eleven courses and call it the *Wiligia* supper because of its proximity to the vigil Mass; the Germans call it *Dickbauch;* the French, *réveillon.* The French and the English light a three-candle candelabra to the honor of the Blessed Trinity.[8]

A common theme is the Christmas loaf, *oblata* in Italian, *oblatky* for Slovaks and *oplatek* for Poles. This is a blessed wafer that occupies a place of honor as a symbol of Christ, the eucharistic Lord. It recalls that God sent manna to his people as they sojourned in the desert and that Jesus has given us himself as "the bread of life" during our earthly journey (John 6:35). The head of the family passes a piece to each member of the family, putting a little honey on it to represent the goodness and gifts of God.

Prayer Before the Christmas Feast (*Roman Ritual*, Appendix)

Priest: The Word was made flesh, alleluia.

All: And dwelt among us, alleluia. Glory be to the Father and to the Son and to the Holy Spirit.

Priest: Bless the Lord.

All: Bless the Lord.

Priest: The poor will eat and receive their fill.

All: Those who seek the Lord will praise him and will live forever. Glory be to the Father and to the Son and to the Holy Spirit.

Priest: Lord, have mercy.

All: Christ, have mercy. Lord, have mercy.

Priest: Our Father,…. And lead us not into temptation.

All: But deliver us from evil.

Priest: Let us pray. Bless us, O Lord, and these your gifts, which we are about to receive from your bounty, through Christ our Lord.

All: Amen.

CHRISTMAS DAY

As we mentioned previously, historically the Christmas tree was set up the night of Christmas Eve, after any children had gone to bed. If it were decorated before then, it would be shut behind locked doors. Andrew's grandfather described the German custom of gathering the family together before the locked doors and unveiling the tree. The parents would light the real candles on the tree, and all would sing carols for the five or seven minutes that the tree remained lit. (Though awed by the beauty of this scene, our lawyers observe that we have in no way endorsed the use of real candles.)

If you decide to buck contemporary practice and save the unveiling of the tree for Christmas morning, have some hymns and gasps of delight on hand to rekindle this expression of Christmas wonder. After the unveiling of the tree comes the most famous of Christmas customs, gift giving, which recalls the gifts of the three wise men over two millennia ago.

CHRISTSTOLLEN

Almost every Christian culture has a special sweetbread dedicated to Christmas. The French bake *brioche*, the Greeks make *melacrino*, and the Germans make *Christstollen*, which Andrew wanted to include here. The *Christstollen* is intended to represent the baby Jesus, as the folds in the dough and white frosting evoke the swaddling clothes in which the newborn was wrapped.

In ages past these festive breads often were blessed by a priest after Mass. Today whoever bakes this representation of Christ might bless it. Lay people do not make a Sign of the Cross over things blessed; the bread is still sprinkled with holy water, however. (Yes, a lay blessing is different from the blessing of the whole Church given by the hands of a priest, but priests deserve a holiday, too.)

As with most of the Christmas cooking, prepare your *stollen* during Advent, allowing everyone time in the days right before Christmas to choose "the good portion" (Luke 10:42). This recipe makes four loaves.

GERMAN CHRISTMAS STOLLEN

- 15 or 16 cups flour

- 1 quart milk

- 4 cakes compressed yeast

- 2 cups sugar

- 1 cup melted shortening

- 1 tablespoon salt

- 1 teaspoon nutmeg

- grated rind of 1 lemon

- 1 pound seedless raisins

- 1/4 pound each slivered citron, candied pineapple, candied cherries, candied orange peel, candied lemon peel

- 1/2 pound blanched almonds, chopped

Sift the flour and measure. Scald milk, and allow to cool to lukewarm. Mix yeast and 1 tablespoon sugar and add to milk. Add 3 cups of flour gradually, beating well with each addition and adding more if necessary. Beat until smooth. Allow sponge to double in bulk.

Add melted shortening, salt, nutmeg, lemon rind, fruit, almonds and remaining sugar and flour. Knead, cover and allow to rise until double in bulk.

Divide into 4 equal parts. Roll each part and pat into a round about 1 inch thick. Crease through the center, brush half with melted butter, fold on crease and press edges together. Brush tops with melted butter. Cover dough and allow to rise until nearly double in bulk.

Bake loaves at 375 degrees for 1 hour. While still warm, cover the tops of the *stollen* with frosting:

- 1-1/2 cups powdered sugar

- 2 tablespoons boiling water

- 2 teaspoons lemon juice

- finely chopped nuts and bits of cherries and angelica

We have no idea what angelica is.

CHRISTSTOLLEN BLESSING (*ROMAN RITUAL*, BLESSING OF BREAD, CHAP. 2, NO. 14C)

Leader: Our help is in the name of the Lord.

All: Who made heaven and earth.

Leader: The Lord be with you.

All: May he also be with you.

Leader: Let us pray. Lord Jesus Christ, bread of angels, true bread of everlasting life, be pleased to bless + this bread, as you once blessed the five loaves in the wilderness, so that all who eat of it may derive health in body and soul. We ask this of you who live and reign forever and ever.

All: Amen.

CHRISTMAS SUGAR COOKIES

As we mentioned above, Christmas cookies have eucharistic origins. Crackers were hung on the Paradise tree to recall the Blessed Sacrament. In time the crackers took on a sweeter taste and became cookies of all shapes and colors.

Christmas at the Salzmanns' wouldn't be Christmas without the amazing varieties of carefully made desserts perfected by Andrew's mother and grandmother. If you're worried about having too many left over—or if you're look-ing for Christmas gifts—follow their example and make up tins of cookies for those on your list. In deference to their eucharistic symbolism, we recommend that you prepare a batch of round, more or less white sugar cookies along with the others; you might even decorate these with eucharistic symbols. Here is a (quite old) Salzmann family recipe:

- 1-1/2 cups sugar
- 1 cup shortening
- 2 eggs
- 1/4 cup sour cream
- 1 teaspoon vanilla
- 1/4 cup nutmeg
- 3 cups flour
- 1/2 teaspoon baking soda
- 1/2 teaspoon salt

Mix sugar into shortening, and cream with eggs, sour cream, vanilla and nutmeg. Stir in flour mixed with baking soda and salt. Mix well. Chill for 1 hour before rolling out dough and cutting cookies. Bake at 400 degrees, 6 to 9 minutes.

Sprinkle with colored sugar or otherwise decorate. Lambs, chalices, grapes, chaffs of wheat, pelicans, monstrances and other eucharistic images are most appropriate.

THE FEAST OF MARY, THE MOTHER OF GOD

In the long view of history, the Church has been less than cel-ebratory on New Year's Day. The peoples of Europe inher-ited a strong tradition of raucous, even scandalous revelry from the Roman Empire, and the Church in the first millennium spent much effort trying to extinguish these elements of sinful indulgence. Bishops forbade the faithful from participating, keeping the day as one of fasting and penance in atonement for their sins. Saint Augustine explained, "During these days, when they [the pagans] revel, we observe a fast in order to cry and pray for them."[9] In Spain the *alleluia* was even omitted at Mass.

When popular raucousness was tamed in the early Middle Ages, the Church continued to celebrate New Year's Day in a spirit of prayer.[10] Given your Saint Sylvester's Day party on New Year's Eve (see chapter six), no one should feel put out by today's more prayerful commemorations.

Perhaps in keeping with this theme of disciplining the flesh, January 1 was formerly the Feast of the Circumcision of the Lord. In the calendar revisions of 1969, it became the Feast of Mary, the Mother of God. Pope Pius XII had consecrated the Church to the special care of the Virgin Mary in 1942. By celebrating the opening of each year with this feast, the Church continues to entrust herself to Mary's care. Entrust your own self to her care in prayer today, asking for her protection in the coming year.

Before the Reformation a custom prevailed of parents blessing their children on special occasions throughout the year. The French brought this custom to French Canada, where it was practiced especially on New Year's Day. Consider following their example. After dinner or family prayers, the father makes the Sign of the Cross on the foreheads of his kneeling family, petitioning the blessing of God for the coming year.[11]

While everyone is kneeling, pick a patron saint for special guidance throughout the coming year. The Scriptures offer us a beautiful image of the saints interceding before God: "Another angel came and stood at the altar with a golden censer; and he was given much incense to mingle with the prayers of all the saints upon the golden altar before the throne" (Revelation 8:3). The body of Christ is truly one body with many members (see 1 Corinthians 12:12), and for this reason Catholics throughout the ages have sought the prayers, the intercession, of holy Christians who have gone before them.

Each member of the family can pick a saint from a basket filled with papers bearing different saints' names. Our experience suggests the process may not be totally random. Often it seems that you do not pick the saint, but the saint picks you!

THE VIGIL OF EPIPHANY

You've heard of the twelve days of Christmas. In a sense they are somewhat of an accident: Throughout ancient Eastern Christianity, January 6 was the important date. The Epiphany to the Magi was celebrated on this day, often simultaneously with the actual birth of Christ and sometimes with other "epiphanies," such as the appearance of the angels to the shepherds. Western Christianity, however, celebrated the feast of Christ's birth on December 25.

In the second half of the fourth century, renewed contacts between Rome and the East resulted in the West's establishing the Feast of Epiphany on January 6, while (most of) the East shifted Christmas to December 25. The twelve days between these two greatly loved feasts became a popular time for parties; they were even referred to as "sacred" by the Second Council of Tours, over fifteen hundred years ago. Join in this tradition and hold your own feast tonight, the "twelfth night of Christmas."

EPIPHANY CAKE

Growing up, Sabitha celebrated Epiphany with a family friend from Belgium, who introduced her to the custom of gathering for a "Three Kings" dessert party. In some countries everyone invited to the party brings a gift, in emulation of the gifts the Magi brought the baby Jesus. The gifts are presented to the Christ child in the manger scene, and then those that can be eaten are enjoyed along with a "twelfth night cake."

The cake may be anything; Sabitha's friend used a chocolate torte. Traditionally a bean is inserted in the cake, though we recommend whatever you deem not to be a legally liable choking hazard. Sabitha's friend used a red M&M. Whoever finds "the bean" in his or her piece of cake becomes king or queen for the year, receiving a crown and a bag of chocolate coins as symbols of the office. Be sure to include other desserts. We bet you still have Christmas cookies.

GOLD, FRANKINCENSE AND MYRRH

The Church provides a special blessing for gold, frankincense and myrrh during Epiphany. After presenting the gifts brought for the party to the Christ child, you might also offer him the same gifts given by the Magi, blessed by a priest after Mass that morning. Our Lord will appreciate these items more than you might suspect. While they seem like odd gifts to give the small child of a modest Hebrew family, they were very symbolic.

Gold, of course, is the offering made to kings, and incense the offering of priests to God; myrrh is a resin used in Roman times for embalming. To offer them again, then, is to proclaim Christ as the rightful king of a world long held captive by the powers of sin, a divine priest who shed his blood for that world's freedom and the prophet killed for proclaiming the reign of God. Obtaining small amounts of these precious items is surprisingly easy: they are often packaged together and sold around Christmas. Check the Internet.

Don't let your pre-party prayer service end without at least one rousing chorus of "We Three Kings," which very effectively recalls the symbolism of the Magi's gifts.

BLESSING OF GOLD, FRANKINCENSE AND MYRRH (*ROMAN RITUAL*, CHAP. 2, NO. 6)

Priest: Our help is in the name of the Lord.

All: Who made heaven and earth.

Priest: The Lord be with you.

All: May he also be with you.

Priest: Let us pray. Accept, holy Father, from me, your unworthy servant, these gifts which I humbly offer to the honor of your holy name and in recognition of your peerless majesty, as you once accepted the sacrifice of the just Abel and the same kind of gifts from the three Magi.

God's creatures, gold, incense, and myrrh, I cast out the demon from you by the Father + almighty, by Jesus + Christ, His only begotten Son, and by the Holy + Spirit, the Advocate, so that you may be freed from all deceit, evil, and cunning of the devil, and become a saving remedy to mankind against the snares of the enemy. May those who use you, with confidence in the divine power, in their lodgings, homes, or on their persons, be delivered from all perils to body and soul, and enjoy all good things. We ask this through the power and merits of our Lord and Savior, the intercession of the Blessed Virgin Mary, Mother of God, and of all the saints, in particular the godly men who on this day venerated Christ the Lord with the very same gifts.

All: Amen.

Priest: God, the invisible and endless One, in the holy and awesome name of your Son, be pleased to endow with your blessing + and power these creatures of gold, incense, and myrrh. Protect those who will have them in their possession from every kind of illness, injury, and danger, anything that would interfere with the well-being of body and soul, and so be enabled to serve you joyously and confidently in your Church; you who live and reign in perfect Trinity, God, forever and ever.

All: Amen.

Priest: And may the blessing of almighty God, + Father, + Son, and Holy + Spirit, come upon these creatures of gold, incense, and myrrh, and remain always.

All: Amen.

The priest sprinkles the gold, frankincense and myrrh with holy water.

EPIPHANY PROCESSION

Once upon a time in the land of Europe, and still today in some regions of Switzerland, the family processed through their home each of the twelve nights of Christmas. In Switzerland these are called the twelve "smoke nights," because the father would lead the procession with blessed incense (or, in a crunch, hay) burning on a shovel to pray for the casting out of demons. (On the advice of our legal counsel, we in no way condone processing through your home while burning straw on a shovel.)

Over the centuries only the final procession—on the vigil of Epiphany—remained popular outside of Switzerland. The procession takes place in the evening, perhaps after dinner. One person leads, carrying a bowl of holy water, which is sprinkled liberally throughout the property, as the rest follow behind, saying the rosary or perhaps singing hymns.

In some places the bishop blesses a special type of holy water for the procession. Known as "Epiphany water," the traditional blessing contains special prayers for deliverance from demonic influence, reflecting the original concern of the twelve "smoke nights." Should Epiphany water be unobtainable, standard-issue holy water is used.

If you want to keep some smoke in your smoke nights, well-stocked Catholic suppliers offer a quite affordable home-sized censer and incense. If you choose to carry candles, we suggest you ensure ahead of time that there is nothing on the floor to trip over. We also suggest you use vigil candles, which come in glass jars, as tapers might drip or burn the faithful.

The procession includes the most celebrated of Epiphany customs, the chalking of the doors. Grandpa Salzmann chalked his doors on Epiphany, and Andrew still remembers the blessing scrawled over the front door. (We don't know that anyone benefited from that blessing: No one was allowed to use the front door.) While chalking wasn't common in Sabitha's household, she became interested in popular piety when she read about this practice online—and the seeds of this book were planted. The practice began in the Middle Ages, as did most things really cool, but remains rather widespread today.

Someone carries a piece of chalk, previously blessed by a priest, in the Epiphany procession. As the group passes doors, particularly ones leading outside, someone (usually the father, in a family context) writes the following on the inside top beam (the lintel) of the door frame: "20 + C + M + B + 08."

The "20" and "08" represent the year in which the chalking is done (2008). The C M B has a dual meaning. First, it implores Christ's blessing by representing the Latin prayer *Christus Mansionem Benedicat,* or "Christ, bless this home." Second, it recalls the traditional names of the three wise men: Caspar, Melchior and Balthasar. Just as these men traveled to the holy house of Nazareth to encounter the Christ child, may this blessing allow all who come to your door to encounter Jesus in the heart of your home.

BLESSING OF THE DOORS BY THE FAMILY

Say this prayer as the doors are chalked:

Prayer for Chalking of the Doors

Leader: The Lord be with you.

All: May he also be with you.

Leader: Let us pray.

Heavenly Father, by a sign in the heavens you called Caspar, Melchior, and Balthasar to worship Jesus Christ, who came to gather the nations of every language for your praise (Isaiah 66:18). In faith, they carried the wealth of the nations—gold, frankincense, and myrrh—to a poor home in Bethlehem. There they encountered the holy child and fell down in worship (Isaiah 66:12, Matthew 2:11).

Father, your Son continues to be the sign sent from heaven, calling all peoples to the true praise of God. Through the ministry of your priest, the Church which praises your name has blessed this chalk, that we might enjoy your favor throughout the year. Call down your blessing upon us, so that all who enter into our home may find Jesus Christ, the treasure of our hearts. Through Christ our Lord.

All: Amen.

The family processes through the home. The leader, traditionally the father, stops at each door to be blessed:

Jesus Christ, you are the door to heaven (John 10:7). By the intercession of Caspar, Melchior and Balthasar, bless this home and all who pass through this door, that they might enter your Father's house, where there are many rooms (John 14:2).

He then writes the initials of the names of the Magi separated by crosses and the year above the door in this manner:

20 + C + M + B + 08

EPIPHANY (JANUARY 6)

On the Feast of Epiphany, the outside world for the first time encountered God made man in the child Jesus, when the wise men found the home at Nazareth. It should not be surprising then that many of the popular customs associated with Epiphany center around the blessing of our homes. If you're not worn out by the party (and prayers) of last night, and if your priest is available, invite him to call down the blessings of the Lord upon your domicile.

Because of the history of "smoke nights," the Church traditionally incensed each room after sprinkling holy water; turn off the smoke detectors and ask Father to bring along the censer. (In past times, when the priest was unable to bless the homes of all the parishioners who requested a blessing, he would say the blessing from the church's steeple, once in each direction.)

Be sure to move the figures of the three kings into your nativity set today. Not only do they represent the Magi recounted in the Gospel of Matthew, but also—depicting as they do three different races—they symbolize the whole of the earth, all the Gentile nations, at last worshipping the God who revealed himself through the chosen people of Israel.

CANDLEMAS (FEBRUARY 2)

The fortieth day after [the Nativity] is indeed celebrated here with the greatest solemnity. On that day, there is a procession into the Anastasis, and all assemble there for the liturgy.... All the priests give sermons, and the bishop, too; and all preach on the Gospel text describing how on the fortieth day Joseph and Mary took the Lord to the temple, and how Simeon and Anna the prophetess...saw Him...and of the offering which His parents brought.

—Egeria the Pilgrim (c. 380)[12]

Technically this feast is called the Presentation of the Lord, like the fourth joyful mystery of the rosary. The Law of Moses commanded that forty days after the birth of the first male child, the mother was to bring him to the temple to present him before God (see Exodus 13:2, 12, 15).

The mother herself was considered ritually unclean, as contact with anything particularly holy (such as the creation of new life: see Leviticus 12:2) or particularly unholy (like unclean food: see Leviticus 11) rendered one ritually unclean. Therefore, she would offer a sacrifice for ritual cleansing—a lamb and a pigeon if the family were rich, two pigeons if the family were poor (Leviticus 12:6, 8). Thus today also has been called the Feast of the Purification of the Blessed Virgin (Luke 2:22–24).

As our faithful adherents to the rosary already know, it was at this presentation that the elderly Anna and Simeon prophesied about Jesus. Simeon proclaimed, "My eyes have seen your salvation / which you have prepared in the presence of all peoples, / a light for revelation to the Gentiles" (Luke 2:30–32). Because of this reference to light, the Church began blessing candles on this day, which is also called "Candlemas," as in "Mass of the Candles."

Make sure to attend Mass today in celebration of the Presentation. Call ahead to see if a Mass will include the initial blessing of candles and Candlemas procession. Bring some of your own candles to be blessed: Catholics use blessed candles for home altars, at bedsides in sickness and during the last rites for the dying, during times of sorrow or temptation or in celebration on feast days and anniversaries. If you are expecting to be expecting, ask your priest to bless a baptismal candle.

CANDLEMAS BREAKFAST

Start your Candlemas off right with crepes, pancakes or eggs; customarily breakfast includes these foods because of their sunny shape.[13] Today is, after all, the celebration of the Christ, Light to the gentiles. You might carry the theme of light over to supper: nothing says "Catholic romance" like a vigil candlelit dinner.

WEATHER FORECASTING

According to the old English proverb: "If Candlemas Day be fair and bright / Winter will have another flight."[14]

Wait. Does that sound vaguely familiar? As with not a few products of the Reformation, Groundhog Day is a secularized banality of an originally Catholic core. The Anabaptist Pennsylvania Dutch who gave us Punxsutawney Phil retained the Germanic custom of weather forecasting on this feast but focused it on gopher shadows. It takes Catholics to make weather forecasting Christocentric.

SOLEMN RECITATION OF THE ROSARY

On the night of this feast, by German custom, everyone would light a new candle and gather around the nativity scene for a solemn recitation of the joyful mysteries. Apparently Germans kept their decorations up longer than we do. After the rosary the father would cut branches from the Christmas tree, one for each family member, on which candy and nuts were still tied. Apparently German kids had a lot more self-discipline than kids we know.

If you barely managed to keep the Christmas tree up through Epiphany, just say the rosary with extra solemnity by candlelight.

LEVANTADO DEL NIÑO

Latin Americans might close off the Christmas season with a Hispanic custom called *Levantado del Niño*. Today they put away the figure of the baby Jesus, which has been on display for over a month. While this seems like a long time to us, the symbolism of displaying the *divino niño* for "only" a month recalls that our relationship is with the *adult* Christ. He entered the world as a baby and often comes into our lives with the same gentleness. But he grew up, as do we, and only as we grow older can we appreciate more fully the redemption of the cross.

To prepare for the *Levantado,* make sure your nativity set is placed such that people can gather around it. If you can, enhance the nativity set by arranging additional pictures of events from the early life of Christ. Break out holy cards or postcards or paintings of the Annunciation, Joseph's vision of the angel, the Visitation, the trip of Mary and Joseph into Bethlehem, their search for lodging, the visit of the Magi to Herod, the adoration of the Magi, the presentation in the temple, Joseph's dream, the flight into Egypt or the massacre of the innocents.

This is not a formal ceremony but a relaxed farewell. Consider reading appropriate passages from Scripture, singing songs or sharing personal reflections. Afterward the figure of the baby Jesus is passed from person to person, and each tells him good-bye in his or her own way. Then baby Jesus is put away for another year.

A warning to those who fail to remove their Christmas wreaths until late August: really, put away the Christmas stuff today. English poet Robert Herrick was annoyed at such laziness and had stern words about it:

Down with the rosemary, and so
Down with the bays and mistletoe;
Down with the holly, ivy, all
Wherewith ye decked the Christmas hall;
That so the superstitious find
No one least branch there left behind:
For look! how many leaves there be
Neglected there, Maids, trust to me
So many goblins you shall see.[15]

English superstition held that homes would be haunted with one devil for each decoration remaining after today.

Chapter Five

Lent and Easter

Depending on the timing of Easter, and on how many of our Christmas suggestions you follow, you might find yourself preparing for Lent even as you put the nativity stuff away. This change was more abrupt before the 1969 calendar revisions, when the Church entered the "pre-Lenten" season perhaps only one week after the end of the Christmas one. The quick change, however, reflects how eager the Church is to share with us the center of our Christian faith: "One has died for all" (2 Corinthians 5:14).

LENT

Offer spiritual sacrifices acceptable to God through Jesus Christ.

—1 PETER 2:5

The Gospels speak of repentance in terms of both turning away from sin and doing penance for sins already committed. Lent is truly a time of repentance in both senses.

One of the most important lenten activities is the continual renunciation of sin; indeed, this is a key Christian activity throughout the year. Atonement for our sins is also solidly part of the gospel message. Saint Peter exhorts us to "make every effort to supplement your faith with virtue, and virtue with knowledge, and knowledge with self-control, and self-control with steadfastness, and steadfastness with godliness, and godliness with brotherly affection, and brotherly affection with love" (2 Peter 1:5–7).

The ways and works that supplement our faith are themselves atonement, as are most especially our acts of love: "Above all hold unfailing your love for one another, since love covers a multitude of sins" (1 Peter 4:8). Our Lord recommends prayer, fasting and almsgiving as means of penance (see Matthew 6:1–18). Lent is unique in its dedication to these three works.

During Lent the whole Christian community follows Christ's example of penance, and from this example the length of Lent is fixed at forty days, not counting Sundays (see Matthew 4:2).

Pretzels are probably the most famous Lenten custom. When eggs and dairy products were forbidden in this season, monks invented this simple treat in the shape of arms folded in prayer. (Hint: Turn them upside down.) But perhaps Lent is one time when tradition and custom should be avoided: This Lent find the spiritual discipline most fitted to the strengths and weaknesses of your Christian life as you live it today.

PALM SUNDAY

"We grant," the heretics say, "that Christ may be represented, but only according to the holy words which we have received from God Himself."…[But Christians] make memorials of His Nativity and [Epiphany]…. We carry branches to represent His sitting on the foal of an ass.

—Saint Theodore the Studite (758-826)[1]

Palm Sunday recalls our Lord's entrance into Jerusalem: At the beginning of Mass on this day, Christ is greeted as King. The liturgical revisions of the last century have joined this commemoration to that of Passion Sunday, so during the Mass we recall how, only a few days after his triumphal entry, our Lord died like a common criminal. This doesn't mean your palms—a symbol of victory—have become meaningless by the end of Mass: it was in the Passion that Christ triumphed over death to become King of our hearts.

As priests like to comment, attendance at Mass is higher when "souvenirs" are handed out. If you are in America, today you will receive a palm branch at Mass. In places where palms are not historically available, as in most of Europe, regional plants like willows may be blessed instead.

These "palms," as the prayers at Mass make clear, are a sign of Christ's victory and kingship. Blessed through the intercession of the whole Church, they are an important sacramental in the home, a continual prayer against the influence of defeated Satan. The palms are either placed behind a crucifix or sacred image or hung in a bundle by the front door.

Whether they received willows or palms, Catholics everywhere have been remarkably skilled at weaving these sacramentals into shapes, particularly that of a cross. Plenty of Web sites offer both simple and quite ambitious weaving suggestions; check them out.

HOLY THURSDAY

This food is called among us [the Eucharist]....We [have] been taught that the food which is blessed by the prayer of His word, and

from which our blood and flesh by transmutation are nourished, is
the flesh and blood of that Jesus who was made flesh.
—Saint Justin Martyr (110–165)[2]

Holy Thursday recalls the Last Supper, the final Passover meal Jesus Christ celebrated with his apostles on the night before he died. Today is also known as Maundy Thursday, from the Latin word for "command," *mandatum*. At this meal Our Lord gave the Church a *new* commandment, "Even as I have loved you, that you also love one another" (John 13:34). On Holy Thursday evening the Mass of the Lord's Supper will recall this command as the celebrant, following Christ's example, washes the feet of twelve parishioners.

It was during the Last Supper that Christ took the bread and wine, blessed them and instituted the memorial of his Body and Blood. The Blessed Sacrament is therefore specially honored by a solemn procession through the church building, moved from its normal tabernacle to a special "altar of repose." Just as Christ invited Peter, James and John to keep vigil with him before his passion (see Mark 14:33–34, 37–38), the Church invites the faithful to keep watch at this altar through the night. The truly hard-core imitate a Roman custom—that of visiting altars of repose at the seven major basilicas—by visiting seven different churches on this night.[3]

In German and Slavic nations, today is often called Green Thursday, or *Gründonnerstag*. The name may have originated from the old German word *grunen*, "to mourn," which eventually degenerated into *grün*, meaning "green."[4] In central Europe the Holy Thursday meal is green, consisting of foods like herb soup, spinach, eggs and ham—which, if they had known Dr. Seuss, would also have been green. Sure, Green Thursday may simply be the result of bad spelling, but use all this green (the liturgical color of hope) for your edification, as a reminder of the promise of salvation that lies beyond the difficult Passion.

If the theological virtue of hope strikes you as too "touchy-feely," get in touch with that old-time religion instead: In pre-Reformation England men shaved their beards on this day as an expression of their grief at the betrayal of Christ, giving rise to the name "Sheer Thursday."[5]

GOOD FRIDAY

For the Word suffered, being in the flesh affixed to the Cross, that He might bring man, who had been deceived by error, to His supreme and godlike majesty, restoring him to that divine life from which he had become alienated.

—Methodius (826–885)[6]

"But, *Mom*, if Jesus *died* today, why's it called '*good*'?!" If you don't remember asking this question, we doubt that you were raised Catholic.

Some Catholic cultures call today "Great Friday," and our English name may be a derivation of this. The Germans call it *Gottesfreitag*, "God's Friday," and "Good Friday" may come from that. But perhaps the most truthful answer comes from Bishop Methodius, quoted above: Today humanity was restored to the divine life of paradise. Yet today is a somber day, recalling the great price of that restoration: the life of our Savior himself.

THE HOUR OF THE PASSION

Good Friday had a somber quality at Sabitha's home, as the family fasted from food and from entertainment that might distract them from the attention that the day demands. Turn off the television and radio, and if possible refrain from work—especially during the hours during which Saint Luke tells us Christ hung on the cross, from noon until three o'clock (see Luke 23:44).

Catholic cultures spend today in quiet contemplation of the sorrows of the Passion, engaged in reflection on the Stations of the Cross and the seven last words of Christ. Attend the Good Friday service at your parish: though today is the only day of the year when Mass is not celebrated, the service includes Holy Communion with hosts reserved from Holy Thursday. A highlight of this service is the veneration of the cross. Those who devoutly adore the crucifix are granted a plenary indulgence (no. 13, s. 1).

PRAYER AT THE HOUR OF THE PASSION (*RACCOLTA*, 204)

Dear Jesus, who for the love of me did hang in agony upon the Cross, and who to complete this great sacrifice embraced the will of your eternal Father, resigning your spirit into His hands, and then bowed your head and died, have pity on all the faithful who are in their agony and upon me; and when I shall come to my latter end, by the merits of your Most Precious Blood give me a perfect conformity to your divine will, so that I may be ready to live or die, as it shall please you; nor do I desire anything else except the perfect fulfillment in me of your adorable will.

HOT CROSS BUNS

Good Friday is a day of fasting and abstinence from meat; in fact, the Irish promoted the custom of a "black fast," consuming nothing but water or black tea. If you're not Irish, today is the traditional day for hot cross buns.

This food caught popular imagination as did few others, inspiring songs and legends. Marked with a cross, the buns were thought to keep away the devil. Even in the nineteenth century, Englishmen would save buns year after year for luck, until they were hard and black with age.[7]

We recommend that you make hot cross buns but that you eat them—preferably with your appropriately meager fare of vegetarian soup and water. Simply add raisins and a little saffron to your favorite bread recipe. Frost a cross on top when cool.

HOLY SATURDAY

Holy Saturday is a day of preparation on both the exterior and interior. The cleaning of homes and the technically optional continuation of the Good Friday fast express the anticipation of the Resurrection. Theologian Hans Urs von Balthasar wrote that Holy Saturday exemplifies the full meaning of the Incarnation. God sent his Son as man into the world; Christ's death and descent into hell demonstrate the "spiritual descent of the Redeemer into the lostness of the sinful heart; the very same [descent] is repeated each time that the Lord goes down into the depths of the *desperata corda* [desperate heart]" hardened by sin.[8]

The Easter Vigil begins on Holy Saturday night. The idea of a vigil has roots in the Old Testament, where God commands Aaron to pray with light and incense in the evening (see Exodus 30:8; Leviticus 24:1–4). It is important to pick up your own candle (with wax-drip protector) as you enter the dark church, as this is crucial to your participation in the liturgy.

The blessing and lighting of the Easter fire begin the liturgy. Saint Patrick gave the bonfire, an originally pagan practice, a Christian meaning in recognizing it as an expression of Christ, the Light of the World.[9] Just like the wise maidens from Saint Luke's parable, we should meet the Lord with our lamps burning.

The paschal candle for the year is blessed and lit from the Easter fire. This candle echoes the imagery of Christ from the prologue of the Gospel of John, "the true light that enlightens every man" and the one who "shines in the darkness" (John 1:9, 5). As the paschal candle is brought to the altar in procession, be sure to have your personal candle in hand. Three times the deacon or priest intones, "Christ our Light," to which we respond, "Thanks be to God." Fire from the paschal candle is used to light everyone's candle, and the dark of the church gives way to light.

The Easter proclamation, the *Exsultet*, is then read. The famous line *O felix culpa*, "O happy fault," references the thought of Saint Augustine of Hippo on Paul's verse, "Where sin increased, grace abounded all the more" (Romans 5:20).[10] The fall of man has resulted in the gift of a great Redeemer.

The vigil continues with the Liturgy of the Word, which consists of nine readings about the meaning of the Passion interspersed with psalm responses. An important part of the vigil is the baptism of catechumens and reception of candidates into full communion in the Church. You'll want to pull out your candle again for the renewal of baptismal promises. The Liturgy of the Eucharist follows.

Those who attend Easter Vigils know that they can go on for hours, depending on the music, the sermon and the number of catechumens and candidates received. Some people still have energy to celebrate the Resurrection immediately afterward with feasting and fellowship.

EASTER SUNDAY

Holy and illustrious Easter, the queen of days, the brilliant night which dissipates the darkness of sin…[today] with abundant light we keep the feast of our salvation, putting ourselves to death along with the Light once put to death for us, and rising again with Him who rose.

—Saint Gregory of Nazianzus (329–389)[11]

Today, in the words of the Mass, "we praise you [God] with greater joy than ever on this Easter day, when Christ became our paschal sacrifice."[12]

The simple fact that we call today *Easter* is a symbol of Christ's victory. Spring was formerly dedicated to Ostara, an Anglo-Saxon goddess.[13] Though Latinate languages use derivations of the Greek word for *Passover* to designate this feast, northern European languages name this time after Ostara, which comes to us as "Easter" in English. Yet it is the victory of Christ that we celebrate today.

NEW CLOTHES

The ritual of baptism ends with the clothing in white garments, in conjunction with Saint Paul's description of "put[ting] on Christ" (Galatians 3:27). Enthusiastic converts in the early Church wore their new white garments to Mass again Easter morning. In time all the faithful began to imitate the catechumens, marking the Resurrection by wearing new clothes for Easter and renewing their baptismal promises.[14] Unlike the early Christians, you don't need to wear your new clothes for the next eight days.

If you're lucky, the Mass for today will feature the Easter sequence *Victimae Paschali* before the Gospel. The sequence, spoken or chanted, tells of Christ's conquest of death and his appearance to Saint Mary Magdalene.

EASTER EGGS, EASTER BASKETS

Easter eggs, whether real, chocolate or jewel-encrusted, are given today from Greece to England to Russia. The Ukrainians are famous for their intricate decorating. They make the eggs predominately red to recall the Precious Blood.

The egg actually has a very clear and significant relation to the Resurrection, representing as it does new life emerging from dark entombment. As for the Easter Bunny, well, that mythical Teutonic hare is really more Ostara's territory.[15] While marshmallow chicks aren't out, consider supplementing candy with food for the soul, like holy cards and small icons. Andrew's Aunt Adeline, growing up in the Depression, recalls bringing their baskets to be blessed at Mass—"to say thanks, I guess."

BLESSING OF FOOD FOR THE FIRST MEAL OF EASTER

God of glory,
>the eyes of all turn to you
>as we celebrate Christ's victory over sin and death.

Bless us and this food of our first Easter meal.
May we who gather at the Lord's table
>continue to celebrate the joy of his resurrection
>and be admitted finally to his heavenly banquet.

Grant this through Christ our Lord.
Amen.[16]

THE FEAST OF FEASTS

Christians of central Europe, particularly the Poles, often had any food eaten on this feast of feasts blessed by a priest on Holy Saturday or Easter itself.[17] Indeed, the *Roman Ritual* includes blessings for lamb, eggs, produce and bread specific to Easter Day. Though the *Roman Ritual* appears to recommend lamb, most of the Easter dinners we've attended featured ham or pork. Most Catholic cultures have special yeast breads for today's feast, reiterating the Resurrection in the rising of bread.

Whatever you serve, show the importance of this day by decorating your table. An image of a lamb is included on Easter tables throughout Catholic Europe, representing the Lamb of God who is risen today. The Poles make their lambs out of butter or pastry dough; the Germans make theirs of kneaded bread; people in both places rest the lamb on a bed of evergreens.[18]

Finish your feast with cheesecake. Cheesecake comes to us from the old English tradition of eating desserts made of milk and honey, representing the fact that Christ's resurrection has won for us the long-awaited Promised Land (see Exodus 3:8).

POLISH EASTER BREAD *(BABA WIELKANOCNA)*

- 2 cups flour
- 1 packet yeast
- 1/2 cup milk
- 1/2 cup margarine
- 1/2 cup sugar
- 3 eggs at room temperature
- 1 cup raisins, seedless

For syrup:

- 1/2 cup brown sugar, boiled
- 1/3 cup water, boiled
- 1/4 cup rum, boiled

Mix 3/4 cup flour and yeast. Combine milk and margarine in a sauce pan, heat till warm only and pour into a bowl. Add yeast and flour mixture, remaining flour and sugar, and beat for 2 minutes with an electric mixer. Add eggs one at a time and up to 1/2 cup flour if necessary to make a thick batter. Beat for an additional 2 minutes. Cover and let rise till doubled.

Stir in raisins, and turn out into a 2-quart greased tube pan. Let rise uncovered for 30 minutes. Bake at 350 degrees for 40 minutes.

Combine syrup ingredients. Before removing bread from

pan and while still hot from the oven, prick with a fork and pour rum syrup over bread.[19]

EASTER MONDAY

After your ridiculously large Easter dinner, you'll probably appreciate a little physical activity. You're in luck: Easter Monday traditionally has been a holiday for pilgrimage, contemplation—and water fights. The Italians call Easter Monday *Pasquetta*, "little Easter," and spend the day playing games, such as rolling a cheese wheel down a hill. The Polish celebrate *Dyngus* Day; in a spirit of joy, the boys drench the girls. Tomorrow the girls have their revenge.

The Gospel traditionally read today describes Christ's appearance to two disciples as they walk the road to Emmaus (see Luke 24:13–35). In an inspiring example of truly taking the Gospel to heart, Christians began taking walks on this day. Meditate on that Scripture passage, enjoy the companionship of your friends and, like the Polish, have a picnic. Your Easter dinner leftovers can serve as a fine meal. A few rolls, some slices of ham, dyed eggs and a few Easter basket goodies will make for a festive meal with minimal effort.

ASCENSION DAY

Through the mystery of the Ascension we, who seemed unworthy of God's earth, are taken up into Heaven.... Our very nature, against which Cherubim guarded the gates of Paradise, is enthroned today high above all Cherubim.

—Saint John Chrysostom (349-407)[20]

The Scriptures tell us that forty days after the Resurrection, Christ ascended to the Father after commissioning his disciples, "Go therefore and make disciples of all nations, baptizing them in the name of the Father and of the Son and of the Holy Spirit, teaching them to observe all that I have commanded you" (Matthew 28:19–20). Christ's ascension therefore falls on the Thursday after the sixth Sunday of Easter, which is celebrated throughout most of the world as a holy day of obligatory Mass attendance, the most important type of feast. Feel free to point this out to your bishop, who has probably chosen to transfer Ascension Thursday to the following Sunday, eliminating the "headache" of attending the eucharistic feast of divine love an extra day of the week. No, we don't understand it either.

THE PENTECOST NOVENA

Did you know that novenas are scriptural? The Ascension and Pentecost happened forty and fifty days after Easter, respectively. Between these two events, Saint Luke tells us, the disciples gathered together in "the upper room" and "with one accord devoted themselves to prayer" (Acts 1:13–14). After nine days of prayer, on the Jewish feast of Pentecost, the Holy Spirit descended on the gathering. Christians ever since have brought important petitions to God in the course of nine days of prayer; hence the Latin word *novena*.

The Pentecost novena begins the day after the Ascension. In the first seven days, meditate on the seven gifts of the Holy Spirit: fear of the Lord, piety, knowledge, fortitude, counsel, understanding and wisdom (see Isaiah 11:2–3). On the eighth day consider the fruits of the Holy Spirit, "love, joy, peace, patience, kindness, goodness, faithfulness, gentleness, [and] self-control" (Galatians 5:22–23). Spend the last day, the ninth, in pious contemplation of the sequence *Veni, Sancte Spiritus* and the hymn *Veni, Creator Spiritus*. Through these nine days in prayerful reflection, one comes to know, love and desire the Holy Spirit more deeply.[21]

PENTECOST

Prayerful preparation is appropriate for the great Feast of Pentecost, the birthday of the Church. In the Old Testament Pentecost was a sort of "Festival of First Fruits." The Israelites hung their homes with garlands and flowers. Eastern Christians did this with roses, and Italians scattered rose petals in their churches. Why rose petals? Perhaps because of their resemblance to the "tongues as of fire" that came to rest on the disciples (see Acts 2:3).

France's celebration had a New Testament base, too, with trumpets blowing like the wind of the Holy Spirit. In England doves were released, before the Reformation killed joviality in religion. If hiring trumpeters seems over the top, continue the festivity at home by spreading rose petals on the dinner table.

Chapter Six

Feasts of Our Lady

One of the most beautiful legacies of the Second Vatican Council is its recovery of the early Church's understanding of Mary. By reminding us of Mary's indivisible connection to the Church, the council made what Pope Benedict XVI has called "one of the most important theological rediscoveries of the twentieth century."[1]

Saint Paul, explaining the redeeming work of Christ's love, explains that our Lord seeks to "present the Church to himself in splendor, without spot or wrinkle or any such thing, that she might be holy and without blemish"—*santa et immaculata* (Ephesians 5:27). The apostle Jude clarifies that the Church Christ redeems is not an abstract thing: The redeeming work of Christ ends when God, "who is able to keep you from falling," will "present you without blemish"—*immaculata*—"before the presence of his glory with rejoicing" (Jude 1:24).

Catholics are accustomed to using this language about Mary. As Saint Ambrose (340–397) explains, "Your example is now the life of Mary, from which shines forth as from a mirror all the beauty" of the Christian life.[2] For the early Church Mary was important not because she is so different from the rest of Christians but because she is the model of what all Christians are called to become.

We discussed the Feast of Mary, the Mother of God, in the fourth chapter, falling as it does in the midst of the Christmas season. Here are several more occasions to keep the Mother of God in your heart and mind. In looking at Mary, the icon of the Church, we glimpse what God has promised we shall become. By celebrating Mary we celebrate the fullness of Christ's redeeming work among us.

THE ANNUNCIATION (MARCH 25)

This is truly the feast of evangelical Christians: the first proclamation of the Good News! Today, exactly nine months before we celebrate the birth of Christ, we mark the angel Gabriel's visit to the Virgin to announce the coming of the Savior. Mary became the perfect model of all Christians by giving her unswerving answer: "Let it be to me according to your word." (Luke 1:38).

WAFFLES

The Annunciation, also known as "Lady Day," is actually the only remaining feast in honor of Mary celebrated in Lutheran Sweden. Today Swedes will feast on waffles at breakfast, lunch or dinner. In addition to being a rich, feast-worthy food in Europe, the waffle was adopted as a reflection of our half-spirited, waffling responses to God, in contrast to the whole-hearted "yes!" of the Blessed Virgin. You might consider illustrating your meal with the figures of Mary and an angel from your nativity set.

EVENING ANGELUS

The Angelus (see p. 28) is perhaps the authors' favorite prayer. It recounts the momentous events celebrated today, the visit of Gabriel and the conception of Christ. Be sure to recite it today, especially the 6 PM Angelus: Gabriel was believed to have appeared to Mary in the evening.

Say the prayer in a large group, if possible, slowly and solemnly. When you get to the words "The Word was made flesh," you might ring some bells to honor the very first moment that the Word of God entered our human existence.

THE ASSUMPTION (AUGUST 15)

They opened the sarcophagus to venerate the precious tabernacle of [Mary] who deserves all praise, but found only her grave-garments; for she had been taken away by Christ.... Jesus Christ himself, who bestowed glory on his immaculate Mother Mary,...will also bestow glory on those who glorify her,... celebrating her memorial every year.

—Saint John of Thessalonica (d. 649)[3]

The oldest feast dedicated specifically to Our Lady, this feast celebrates Mary's entrance into eternal life. Originating in Palestine, the feast spread throughout the whole East in 602 by decree of Emperor Mauritius. Almost immediately Rome followed suit.[4]

The feast originally celebrated "the falling asleep of Mary"—her death, often more delicately termed her "dormition." Unique among all the saints, Our Lady entered heaven not simply in soul, awaiting the resurrection of her dead body, but rather in both soul and body. Mary, a symbol of the whole Church, has already received the fullness of salvation—body and soul—that all the saints anticipate.

In the United States the Feast of the Assumption is perhaps best known as "that one holy day of obligation in late summer." Old Europe celebrated the Assumption much more intensely: For Eastern Christians the feast is preceded by a short version of Lent, two weeks of fasting and penance. Sicilians echo the older Eastern practice by fasting from fresh fruit for those two weeks; on the feast itself, fruit is blessed at church, and people exchange fruit baskets—a gift you don't have to be Sicilian to appreciate.[5]

In Poland and Germany herbs or regular flowers are also blessed today. Like the flavoring herbs, the sweetness of Mary's sanctity adds joy to our lives. Subsequently the herbs become reminders of the heavenly destiny we share with Our Lady each time we cook with them.

BLESSING OF HERBS ON THE FEAST OF THE ASSUMPTION (*ROMAN RITUAL*, CHAP. 2, NO. 17)

Immediately before Mass the priest stands before the altar facing the people, who hold up their herbs and fruits. The prayer is from Psalms 65, 104 and 107.

Priest: Our help is in the name of the Lord.

All: Who made heaven and earth.

Priest: To you we owe our hymn of praise, O God, in Sion; to you must vows be fulfilled, you who hear prayers.

All: To you all flesh must come / because of wicked deeds.

Priest: We are overcome by our sins; / it is you who pardon them.

All: Happy the man you choose, / and bring to dwell in your courts.

Priest: May we be filled with the good things of your house, / the holy things of your temple.

All: With awe-inspiring deeds of justice you answer us, / O God our Savior,

Priest: The hope of all the ends of the earth / and of the distant seas.

All: You set the mountains in place by your power, / you who are girt with might;

Priest: You still the roaring of the seas, / the roaring of their waves and the tumult of the peoples.

All: And the dwellers at the earth's ends are in fear at your marvels; / the farthest east and west you make resound with joy.

Priest: You have visited the land and watered it; / greatly have you enriched it.

All: God's watercourses are filled; you have prepared the grain. / Thus have you prepared the land:

Priest: Drenching its furrows, / breaking up its clods,

All: Softening it with showers, / blessing its yield.

Priest: You have crowned the year with your bounty, / and your paths overflow with a rich harvest;

All: The untilled meadows overflow with it, / and rejoicing clothes the hills.

Priest: The fields are garmented with flocks and the valleys blanketed with grain. / They shout and sing for joy.

All: Glory be to the Father…

Priest: As it was in the beginning,…

Priest: The Lord will be gracious.

All: And our land will bring forth its fruit.

Priest: You water the mountains from the clouds.

All: The earth is replenished from your rains.

Priest: Giving grass for cattle.

All: And plants for the benefit of man.

Priest: You bring wheat from the earth.

All: And wine to cheer man's heart.

Priest: Oil to make his face lustrous.

All: And bread to strengthen his heart.

Priest: He utters a command and heals their suffering.

All: And snatches them from distressing want.

Priest: Lord, heed my prayer.

All: And let my cry be heard by you.

Priest: The Lord be with you.

All: May he also be with you.

Priest: Let us pray. Almighty everlasting God, who by your word alone brought into being the heavens, earth, sea, things seen and things unseen, and garnished the earth with plants and trees for the use of man and beast; who appointed each species to bring forth fruit in its kind, not only for the food of living creatures, but for the healing of sick bodies as well; with mind and word we urgently call on you in your great kindness to bless + these various herbs and fruits, thus increasing their natural powers with the newly given grace of your blessing. May they keep away disease and adversity from men and beasts who use them in your name; through Christ our Lord.

All: Amen.

Priest: Let us pray. God, who through Moses, your servant, directed the children of Israel to carry their sheaves of new grain to the priests for a blessing, to pluck the finest fruits of the orchard, and to make merry before you, the Lord their God; hear our supplications, and shower blessings + in abundance upon us and upon these bundles of new grain, new herbs, and this assortment of produce which we gratefully present to you on this festival, blessing + them in your name. Grant that men, cattle, flocks, and beasts of burden find in them a remedy against sickness, pestilence, sores, injuries, spells, against the fangs of serpents or poisonous creatures. May these blessed objects be a protection against diabolical mockery, cunning, and deception wherever they are kept, carried, or otherwise used. Lastly, through the merits of the Blessed Virgin Mary, whose Assumption we are celebrating, may we all, laden with the sheaves of good works, deserve to be taken up to heaven; through Christ our Lord.

All: Amen.

Priest: Let us pray. God, who on this day raised up to highest heaven the rod of Jesse, the Mother of your Son, our Lord Jesus Christ, that by her prayers and patronage you might communicate to our mortal nature the fruit of her womb, your very Son; we humbly implore you to help us use these fruits of the soil for our temporal and everlasting welfare, aided by the power of your Son and the prayers of his glorious Mother; through Christ our Lord.

All: Amen.

Priest: And may the blessing of almighty God, Father, Son, + and Holy Spirit, come upon these creatures and remain always.

All: Amen.

The priest sprinkles with holy water and incenses the congregation.

THE IMMACULATE CONCEPTION (DECEMBER 8)

The Faith has ever been my guide, and has given me to eat a fish, a great and pure fish, which a spotless [immaculata] *virgin drew forth.*

—Abercius of Phrygia (c. 190)[6]

Many Catholics mistake the meaning of this feast, a holy day of obligation in the United States, for the virginal conception of Christ. The Gospel reading, which is the Annunciation, helps to fuel this misunderstanding. The focus, however, is on the angel Gabriel's words describing Mary as "full of grace." This feast celebrates Mary's conception without the guilt of original sin in preparation for her role as God-bearer. Should all that theology sound too highfalutin, read the story of the peasant girl Saint Bernadette, with whom Our Lady of Lourdes shared this doctrine.

The Church grants a partial indulgence to the faithful who take part in a public novena before the Feast of the Immaculate Conception (no. 22, s. 1). The last day should fall on the day before the feast.

NOVENA (*RACCOLTA*, 371)

O pure and immaculate and likewise blessed Virgin, you who are the sinless Mother of your Son, the mighty Lord of the universe, you who are inviolate and altogether holy, the hope of the hopeless and sinful, we sing your praises. We bless you, as full of every grace, you who did bear the God-Man: we all bow low before you; we invoke you and implore your aid. Rescue us, O holy and inviolate Virgin, from every necessity that presses upon us and from all the temptations of the devil. Be our intercessor and advocate at the hour of death and judgment; deliver us from the fire that is not extinguished and from the outer darkness; make us worthy of the glory of your Son, O dearest and most clement Virgin Mother. You indeed are our only hope most sure and sacred in God's sight, to whom be honor and glory, majesty and dominion for ever and ever world without end. Amen.

MARY CANDLE

On the day of the feast itself, consider lighting a Mary Candle, an old German custom. During the whole period of Advent, a candlestick is clothed in white silk to represent the purity of the immaculate Mother from whom came the Light of the World. This candle is lit during family prayers each night. Take a cue from Our Lady of Lourdes, who appeared in a white robed lined with blue stripes. On the day of the feast, adorn the silk with some blue ribbon.[7]

OUR LADY OF GUADALUPE (DECEMBER 12)

A priest we know once received a phone call from the local Methodist church. "You have such success with Latinos!" the speaker exclaimed. "How can we reach out to them, too?" Taking a breath, Father explained the eucharistic presence, novenas to Saint Anthony and devotion to Our Lady of Guadalupe, dear to many Hispanics.

Indeed, the Church owes the success she has had spreading the Word of God in Mexico to the Mother of God, who appeared there famously as Our Lady of Guadalupe. When Pope John Paul II visited Mexico in 1999, he remarked that about 80 percent of Mexico was Catholic, but all Mexicans were devoted to Our Lady of Guadalupe.

Immediately after the Spanish conquest of the Americas, the native peoples were (not surprisingly) uninterested in the religion of their conquerors. Franciscan missionaries from Spain struggled to spread the gospel with little fruit. Then Mary intervened.

Juan Diego, one of the few early native converts to the Church, was on his way to Mass on December 9, 1531, when he saw an apparition of Mary dressed as an Aztec woman. Our Lady told him that she was his mother, and she asked for a church to be built on the site, the hill of Tepeyac, near Mexico City. Juan went to his bishop, who requested a sign of supernatural involvement.

Juan Diego conveyed this message to Mary at the next apparition, and she in turn promised a sign at the same place the next day. But Juan Diego took a different road the next morning because he had to summon a priest to minister to his uncle, who was ill. Our Lady appeared to him nonetheless, placing roses in his cactus-skin cloak.

Juan Diego took the bundle of roses to the bishop in accordance with Our Lady's wishes. When he unrolled his cloak, the roses fell away to reveal a miraculous image of Our Lady. Nearly five hundred years later, the cloak of Juan Diego is still intact, despite the frailty of cactus skin (which typically has a lifespan of twenty to thirty years) and a twentieth-century bombing of the image. The image seems miraculously imposed on the cloth, called the *tilma,* neither painted on nor woven into the cloth; many of its details continue to baffle science.

The apparition lives on in other ways. Aztec human sacrifices ended following the conversion of Mexico. This, plus

ANALYZING THE IMAGE OF OUR LADY OF GUADALUPE

Mary always points to Jesus. The iconography of Guadalupe is no different.

Aztec woman	The "foreign" gospel has become native
Eyes down	She is not God
Stars	Constellation pattern in December 1531
Maternity band	Pregnant with the Savior
Pupils	Contain microscopic inverted images of Juan Diego
Sun and moon	"A woman clothed with the sun, with the moon under her feet" (Revelation 12:1)
Castilian roses	These Spanish flowers grow neither in winter nor in Mexico, yet Juan Diego presented them to the bishop

the fact that Our Lady of Guadalupe appeared as a pregnant woman, caused Pope John Paul II to name her the patroness of the unborn. He also canonized Juan Diego in 2002. In 1946 Pope Pius XII had named Our Lady of Guadalupe the Patroness of the Americas.

Friends tell us that many Mexicans begin December 12 in the Basilica of Our Lady of Guadalupe, serenading the Lord and Our Lady before the *tilma* with the song *"Las Mañanitas."* After you've sung to Our Lady today, recall her protection of the unborn and her assistance to their mothers. Consider serving traditional Mexican food, such as mole, enchiladas or fajitas. Have a pro-life dessert: *Churros* and Mexican hot chocolate would increase anyone's zeal for living.

Chapter Seven

Feasts of Other Saints

A pple *kuchen*." Grandpa Salzmann smiled. "Mother always made apple *kuchen* on Saint Sylvester's day."

Often modern Americans only encounter religious folk customs through the lens of anthropological study; "culture day" in Spanish class might be the closest many get to celebrating any pious practices. But with this passing memory, Andrew's grandfather introduced an entire world of religious traditions celebrated by American Catholics only a few decades ago. This chapter (our favorite) presents a few of those popular customs long used to celebrate and honor the saints.

We have all heard of "red letter days." The phrase comes from Christian worship: Important feasts were printed in missals using red ink. Catholics can lay claim to many common words and phrases: "lukewarm" (Saint Luke's day tended to be unseasonably warm), "cappuccino" (it's brown, like a Capuchin's habit) and *sacre bleu!* (an invocation of Mary's "sacred blue" cloak). "Red-letter days," however, is Anglican in origin. In another sweeping gesture of ecumenism, we will nonetheless employ it here.

The Church celebrates the memory of at least one saint, and sometimes dozens, each day of the year. In this chapter we'll highlight a few "red-letter days," saintly celebrations rich with Catholic traditions. But we'll also suggest ways in which to celebrate other feasts for saints to whom you might be devoted but who are not mentioned here.

SAINT BLAISE (FEBRUARY 3)

Saint Blaise was the bishop of Sebaste, Armenia, until his martyrdom in 317. Many miracles are attributed to him, both by Eastern and Western Christians, but the most famous is his cure of a young boy choking on a fishbone; for this reason we continue to call upon his intercession for throat ailments and for good health in general.

According to another legend Saint Blaise once encountered a poor woman whose only pig had been consumed by a wolf. At his command the wolf restored the pig, alive, to its owner. (Admittedly, the historical accuracy of this account is unconfirmed.) Later, when the bishop was imprisoned before his martyrdom, the same woman brought him candles to light the dank cell.[1] This has been suggested as the reason candles are used in the blessing of throats today; a more likely reason may be that yesterday was Candlemas.

THE BLESSING OF THROATS

Saint Blaise became wildly popular in the Middle Ages, and even now on his feast the Church gives a special blessing of the throat. The priest makes an X with two blessed candles, places them against an individual's throat and recites the prayer, "Through the intercession of Saint Blaise, bishop and martyr, may God deliver you from every disease of the throat, and from every other disease. In the name of the Father, and of the Son and of the Holy Spirit."[2] This blessing is yours for the asking after Mass on this feast. Some churches provide it at the Sunday Mass within the week of the feast.

PAN BENDITO

The woman who brought Saint Blaise candles in the night was also said to have brought him dinner in jail. Perhaps related to this, a lesser known custom of blessing food prevails in Italy. The blessed food (bread, wine, water or fruit) is then distributed to people who either eat it or, more traditionally, store it away. They then invoke Saint Blaise's intercessory prayers by eating a small piece of the blessed food when next their throats are sore.

If this were simply food, of course, the practice should be dismissed as superstitious. However, the food is a sacramental in light of its blessing. In eating it the faithful depend on the prayer of the Church for healing, not the food itself.

BLESSING OF FOOD IN HONOR OF SAINT BLAISE (ROMAN RITUAL, CHAP. 2, NO. 11)

Priest: Our help is in the name of the Lord.

All: Who made heaven and earth.

Priest: The Lord be with you.

All: May he also be with you.

Priest: Let us pray. God, Savior of the world, who consecrated this day by the martyrdom of blessed Blaise, granting him among other gifts the power of healing all who are afflicted with ailments of the throat; we humbly appeal to your boundless mercy, begging that these fruits, bread, wine, and water brought by your devoted people be blessed + and sanctified + by your goodness. May those who eat and drink these gifts be fully healed of all ailments of the throat and of all maladies of body and soul, through the prayers and merits of Saint Blaise, bishop and martyr. We ask this of you who live and reign, God, forever and ever.

All: Amen.

The priest sprinkles the food with holy water.

SAINT PATRICK (MARCH 17)

Saint Patrick was, as any Catholic should know, the "apostle of Ireland," the man sent by Pope Celestine to convert that country to the faith. He labored extensively for three decades in the face of fierce opposition from Druidic priests, dying in the year 461.

Because of the great Irish heritage in America, Saint Patrick's Day is enthusiastically celebrated with leprechauns and excessive quantities of green beer. Neither of these, however, fall into the category of popular piety. (Truly devout Catholics drink Guinness.)

SHAMROCKS

Today you will see many four-leaf clovers. True shamrocks, however, have only three leaves. These are associated with Saint Patrick because, according to legend, he used one to explain the doctrine of the Holy Trinity to the pagan King Oengus.[3] (One plant, three leaves; get it?)

Irish men traditionally wear the shamrock on their hats, and women wear a cross made of ribbon on their dresses. This practice is reflected in what we are told is an Irish saying, "A shamrock on every hat, low and tall, and a cross on every girl's dress," though it doesn't sound like much of a saying to us.[4]

Although not used by Saint Patrick, four-leaf clovers are also related to the symbolism of the traditional shamrock: Three of the leaves are said to represent the Holy Trinity, with the fourth symbolizing the grace of God, by which we "become partakers of the divine nature" (2 Peter 1:4). It is speculated that this symbolism lies behind the conception that four-leaf clovers are lucky.

BLESSING OF BEER (*ROMAN RITUAL*, CHAP. 8, NO. 5)

For Patrick's sake, not green beer!

> Priest: Our help is in the name of the Lord.
>
> All: Who made heaven and earth.
>
> Priest: The Lord be with you.
>
> All: May he also be with you.
>
> Priest: Let us pray. Lord, bless + this creature, beer, which by your kindness and power has been produced from kernels of grain, and let it be a healthful drink for mankind. Grant that whoever drinks it with thanksgiving to your holy name may find it a help in body and in soul; through Christ our Lord.
>
> All: Amen.
>
> *The priest sprinkles the beer with holy water.*

SAINT JOSEPH (MARCH 19)

Today is the first of two feasts in honor of Saint Joseph, spouse of the Virgin Mary and foster father of our Lord. On May 1 we honor him particularly as the patron of workers.

With altars dedicated to Mary and Joseph common in almost every older American church, who would have guessed that devotion to Saint Joseph has been widespread for only about five hundred years? Pilgrims to the Holy Land brought devotion to Joseph back to Europe from Eastern Christianity around the time of the Crusades. The Carmelites —who originated at this time in the Holy Land—and their famous daughter Saint Teresa of Avila had the largest role in popularizing Saint Joseph.

Devotion to Joseph, especially as the head of the Holy Family, has affirmed a positive spirituality of marriage and the lay vocation throughout the Catholic world. As head of the Holy Family, it was Saint Joseph's responsibility to put bread on the, er, holy table. Not surprisingly, popular customs on this feast revolve largely around feeding families.

SAINT JOSEPH'S TABLE

Sicilian Christians traditionally create elaborate tables or "altars" in honor of Saint Joseph, where they place offerings of food for the homeless. Because these tables form an intensely Catholic sort of food drive, we recommend pooling resources: Get many households or even your whole parish to participate. Your priest can use the special blessing for these altars found in the current edition of the *Book of Blessings*.

Organize your Saint Joseph altar carefully. If possible, arrange tables in the shape of a cross, with the head against a wall. This back portion of the altar climaxes in three progressively smaller levels, representing the Trinity. Cover the whole altar with white cloth.[5] Place on the top level a statue of Saint Joseph or perhaps the Holy Family. On the second level you might include memorials to the deceased, flowers, statues of other saints and votive candles.

The lowest level, the surface of the tables, is for the donations for the poor. Traditionally these included many items prepared in the home, but today most food kitchens prefer packaged foods. Place a basket on the altar to receive petitions to Saint Joseph as well as monetary donations for the poor.[6]

SAINT JOSEPH'S MEAL

Saint Joseph's Day falls during Lent, and so, though it is enthusiastically celebrated, traditional foods for the day are meatless. Typical Italian dishes include minestrone, *cioppino* (fish stew), spinach-stuffed pasta shells, pasta with garbanzo beans and baked fish.[7] A common staple of the feast is Pasta Milanese, which features a tomato sauce flavored with sardines. The entrée is sprinkled with *mudrica*, grated stale bread, which not only resembles the sawdust of Saint Joseph's workshop but also harks back to a stricter observance of Lent, when animal products such as the typical Parmesan cheese topping were given up.[8]

Despite Lent, enjoy the Italian dessert especially dedicated to Joseph's feast, *zeppole*, which can be purchased at an Italian bakery in the days around his feast. Cakes, breads and cookies honoring the Holy Family's breadwinner abound, decorated with or shaped as religious symbols, such as Saint Joseph's flowering staff or lily.[9] Follow custom and set a statue of the saint at the table to preside over your familial feast.

GARDENING

Andrew's Aunt Adeline recalls that Saint Joseph's day was supposed to be the lucky day to start seedlings for the garden. Questions of luck aside, it's easy to see why the gardens that fed families were placed under Joseph's protection. A more "high church" beginning of spring was celebrated in Europe, where candles and shrines to Joseph were erected in gardens and orchards.[10]

In planting your seedlings you'll want to think ahead to other feasts. Consider planting Saint-John's-wort to celebrate the birth of Saint John on June 24 and Michaelmas daisies (known as New York asters in some areas) to place on your home altar on the Feast of Saints Michael, Gabriel and Raphael on September 29.

BLESSING OF SEED (*ROMAN RITUAL,* CHAP. 8, NO. 10)

Priest: Our help is in the name of the Lord.

All: Who made heaven and earth.

Priest: The Lord be with you.

All: May he also be with you.

Priest: Let us pray. Lord, we earnestly beg you to bless + these seeds, to protect and preserve them with gentle breezes, to make them fertile with heavenly dew, and to bring them, in your benevolence, to the fullest harvest for our bodily and spiritual welfare; through Christ our Lord.

All: Amen.

The priest sprinkles the seeds with holy water.

SAINT GEORGE (APRIL 23)

Saint George was a fourth-century Roman soldier martyred for the faith. The medievals held that one day George happened to enter a town harassed by a horrible dragon. To quell the dragon's wrath, every day the citizens were compelled to sacrifice a goat and a child. Unaware of this situation, George asked a troubled young princess what bothered her, only to discover that she was the day's sacrificial victim. George captured the dragon by using the princess's garter, and he offered to free the town of its bondage to the dragon upon their baptism.[11]

Dragon or no, the figure of Saint George is historical: Born in the fourth century, he was martyred under the Emperor Diocletian in Nicodemia, Turkey.[12] If the legend is the thinly veiled allegory it appears to be, he well may have ended the area's bondage to the dragon of sin through his ministry of the saving waters of baptism.

Saint George is supposed to have appeared to the Crusaders, assisting them in the siege of Jerusalem. Indeed, upon the return of the Crusaders to England, Saint George became that nation's patron saint. In his honor were founded the Knights of the Garter, and in times past Britons would don blue coats on this day in imitation of the blue mantle worn by these knights.[13] Others would wear a red rose in honor of George and England.

The Russians, at least in times past, held special dinners on this day to honor veterans and military men, for whom Saint George is the patron.[14] Consider having a dinner to honor the chivalrous men in your life. Sabitha, who was born in England, recommends some traditional English soup. You might round the meal out with fish and chips.

SABITHA'S CARROT GINGER SOUP (FOR TWO)

- 3 carrots, peeled and sliced
- 1 1/2 cups water

- 1/2 cup golden raisins
- 1 tablespoon grated ginger
- 1 teaspoon cinnamon
- 1/2 teaspoon *garam masala* or curry powder

Boil the carrots in the water until tender. Remove from heat and run through blender. Return to heat. Add raisins and spices. Simmer until the raisins are plump, about 30 minutes.

SAINT MARK (APRIL 25)

Saint Mark the evangelist is believed to be the disciple who ran away after Christ's arrest in the Garden of Gethsemane (see Mark 14:51–52). Young at the time of the crucifixion, he helped spread Christianity extensively before his martyrdom. He was Saint Peter's secretary, assisting him in Rome, where his Gospel may have been written (see 1 Peter 5:13).

Eventually Mark became bishop of Alexandria, Egypt. While presiding at the Eucharist on Easter Sunday, he was arrested and dragged through the streets to his death. A hailstorm caused his assailants to abandon his body, which his disciples rescued for veneration.[15]

In the ninth century Mark's relics were translated (read: looted) to the church of San Marco in Venice. Within two centuries the Venetians had forgotten where they had entombed the relics. Petitioning divine assistance with a rigorous Triduum fast, the column in which they had been deposited miraculously split apart.[16]

Because his feast coincides with the former Major Rogation days—days of prayer and petition—Saint Mark's feast included the Rogation procession. In Venice this procession has been held in his basilica. Venetian men give a red rose, or *bocolo*, to their sweethearts today, recalling the aroma of roses that filled the air when Mark's relics were found in 1094.[17]

Several foods are associated with Saint Mark's day. The Venetians make a risotto with fresh peas called *risi con bisi*. Serve it with Saint Mark's bread. *Marci panis* in Latin, you may know this Bavarian food by its more common name, *marzipan*.[18] The recipe is fussy; buy some from your grocery store instead. Try creating Mark's symbol, the lion, in the almond paste. Early Christians, reading the Book of Revelation, recognized the "four living creatures" to be the four Gospel writers (see Revelation 4:6–7). They attributed the lion to Mark because his Gospel begins with John the Baptist, a "voice of one crying out" like a lion in the desert (Mark 2:1).

THE APOSTLES PHILIP AND JAMES THE LESSER (MAY 3)

"Every one who calls upon the name of the Lord will be saved." But how are men to call upon him in whom they have not believed? And how are they to believe in him of whom they have never heard? And how are they to hear without a preacher? And how can men preach unless they are sent?

—ROMANS 10:13–15

The credibility of any message is rooted in the person who sent it. A check for a million dollars, for example, is more or less credible depending upon whether the return address label reads "IRS" or "Publishers' Clearing House." Andrew once explained this problem of credibility to some missionaries who appeared at the door, excited to share a religion that was organized 150 years ago but claimed Cain as its founder. The historical record simply does not show that anyone believed their claims until very recently.

The credibility of the Catholic Church and its proclamation of the cross of Christ rests on the modern bishop, who sends his priests and faithful out into the world. The modern bishop's credibility, in turn, depends on the constant line of two thousand years of bishops preceding him, beginning with the apostles who sent them and who alone were sent by Jesus Christ (see Matthew 28:16–20).

CROSSES IN THE FIELDS

On this feast celebrating the credibility of our apostolic faith, "preach Christ crucified!" (1 Corinthians 1:23). Before the Reformation today was the Feast of the Holy Cross of Christ, and the faithful erected crosses publicly—in vineyards, fields and so on. This custom has outlived the feast that inspired it. Now we celebrate two apostles who proclaimed the love Christ showed on the cross. Join them in spreading the Good News by erecting a cross in your yard.

Prayer for the Setting Up of Crosses Outdoors

Leader: The Lord be with you.

All: May He also be with you.

Leader: Let us pray.

Almighty Father, you raised up our Lord Jesus Christ upon the cross, so that he might draw all people to himself. (John 12:32) For this reason, you sent James to proclaim

Christ crucified in the holy city of Jerusalem, and you entrusted Philip with the knowledge that whosoever sees the Son has seen you, the Father. (John 14:9)

In ancient times, you commanded that Moses hold aloft the bronze serpent, so that by looking at the sign of their affliction the Israelites might be healed from the bite of these snakes. (Numbers 21:9) Grant, we ask you, that all who look upon these images of your crucified Son, placed in fields and gardens, might turn away from sin by beholding the affliction of Jesus Christ, who for our sakes was made to be sin. (2 Corinthians 5:21)

We ask this through Christ our Lord.

All: Amen.

SAINT ANTHONY OF PADUA (JUNE 13)

Son of Lisbon's chief magistrate, Saint Anthony grew up accustomed to courtly surroundings. Called to the priesthood rather than knighthood, he eventually became one of the first Franciscans. He was assigned to minister to the people of Padua, and he converted the city to a deeper love of Christ. The people of Padua loved him in return.

Through his example, his instruction and a myriad of miracles, Anthony fought immorality and heresy throughout Italy and France. Sabitha was able to see his incorrupt tongue—proof of his preaching prowess—at his basilica in Padua. Anthony was canonized within a year of his death in 1231.[19]

SAINT ANTHONY'S LILIES

You thought we were going to tell you to pray to Saint Anthony to find your lost car keys! Most Catholics are aware that this saint's courtly manners persist in heaven, and as patron of lost items, he patiently assists thousands of frantic Christians each day. But we're going to talk about lilies, a traditional symbol of purity.

Saint Anthony famously enjoyed a vision of the Christ child coming to rest in his arms; hence with Saint Joseph, he is one of two men depicted holding the infant Jesus.[20] Because "the pure of heart...shall see God," the lily is the symbol of both (Matthew 5:8).

When your lilies bloom, pick out the brown, powdery pods in the blossoms immediately, lest the powder stain everything in sight. Often these lilies are dried, like palm branches, so as to take advantage of the Church's prayer of blessing year-round. This is no mean feat. Fill a bucket taller than the lily halfway with sand, and place the lily upright in the sand. Fill the bucket to the top, covering the lily completely. Careful pouring is necessary: the sand should help the lily retain its shape, not crush it.

BLESSING FOR LILIES (*ROMAN RITUAL*, CHAP. 7, NO. 23)

Priest: Our help is in the name of the Lord.

All: Who made heaven and earth.

Priest: The Lord be with you.

All: May he also be with you.

Priest: Let us pray. God, the Creator and preserver of the human race, the lover of holy purity, the giver of supernatural grace, and the dispenser of everlasting salvation; bless + these lilies which we, your humble servants, present to you today as an act of thanksgiving and in honor of Saint Anthony, your confessor, and with a request for your blessing. Pour out on them, by the saving sign + of the holy cross, your dew from on high. You in your great kindness have given them to man, and endowed them with a sweet fragrance to lighten the burden of the sick. Therefore, let them be filled with such power that, whether they are used by the sick, or kept in homes or other places, or devoutly carried on one's person, they may serve to drive out evil spirits, safeguard holy chastity, and turn away illness—all this through the prayers of Saint Anthony—and finally impart to your servants grace and peace; through Christ our Lord.

All: Amen.

The priest sprinkles the lilies with holy water, saying:

Sprinkle me with hyssop, Lord, and I shall be clean of sin. Wash me, and I shall be whiter than snow. Pray for us, Saint Anthony.

All: That we may be worthy of Christ's promise.

Priest: Let us pray. We beg you, O Lord, that your people may be helped by the constant and devout intercession of Blessed Anthony, your illustrious confessor. May he assist us to be worthy of your grace in this life, and to attain everlasting joys in the life to come; through Christ our Lord.

All: Amen.

After this the lilies are distributed to the people.

THE BIRTH OF JOHN THE BAPTIST (JUNE 24)

I say to you, among those born of women there has arisen no one greater than John the Baptist.

—MATTHEW 11:11

Usually the Church celebrates the deaths of saints—that is, their birth into eternal life. The only earthly births celebrated are those of Jesus, Mary and John the Baptist. While not divine like our Lord or immaculate in heart like Our Lady, the Church teaches that John holds a special place in salvation history as the "pre-sanctified" herald of Christ, "filled with the Holy Spirit, / even from his mother's womb" (Luke 1:15).

Saint Augustine mentions this belief as a widespread conviction in fourth-century Christianity.[21] Indeed, John once had a far greater place in the Christian imagination than we might imagine. Priest and theologian Louis Bouyer calls John's post-Reformation fall into virtual oblivion "startling," lamenting that Saint John "is a central figure in the whole economy of the Mystery, as is still shown by the place he has retained in the liturgy, and if we leave him out, we are in danger of losing the whole meaning of the [Christian] Mystery itself."[22] John's radical response to the advent of the Lamb of God has made him the exemplar of monastic life and an inspiration to all Christians.

Because John's birthday is the summer solstice, the days now will begin to grow shorter, whereas the days after Christ's birthday begin to lengthen. Hence the cosmic cycle echoes John's statement about Jesus, "He must increase, but I must decrease" (John 3:30).

SAINT JOHN'S WREATHS

In more Catholic times doors in England were decorated today with wreaths of Saint-John's-wort. Perhaps the best way to make a wreath from a plant with the structural integrity of a weed is to begin with a frame. Take simple wire (thicker is better: we recommend 14-gauge general purpose), and make a circle of any size; four inches in diameter is nice. Wrap the wire around itself, completing as many rotations as necessary to provide a foundation.

Next, if you didn't plant Saint-John's-wort on Saint Joseph's day, you will need to obtain some. The plant is a rather common weed; find a picture of it online, take a walk and gather a judicious amount. You will be less frustrated if you pick off some of the flowers in advance, wrap the stalks around the frame and then insert the flowers into the finished wreath for maximum visibility.

SAINT JOHN'S BONFIRE

The English language, we regret to inform you, has pagan origins; yet Christians use it to preach and praise the Word of God. The same can be said of Saint John's bonfire: prevalent all across Europe, from the heights of the Alps to the plains of the Ukraine, these fires have their roots in the pagan *nied-fyr*, or "need fire," lit on the solstice in pre-Christian times to cleanse the earth from evil and cure malevolent disease.[23] Since the rise of Christianity, these fires have been lit instead as a fitting tribute to John, who "came for testimony, to bear witness to the light, that all might believe through him" (John 1:7).

The fire is customarily lit with a blessed candle while someone reads a poem in the saint's honor. The fire itself is then blessed, and hymns in honor of the saint are sung. One of these, *Ut queant laxis*, is the origin of denoting musical notes as "do, re, mi, fa, so, la, ti."

Ask Saint John's intercession for summer blessings in homes, fields and country. European Christians enjoy jumping over the fire, but our lawyers firmly recommend that you find safer ways to enjoy your bonfire.

BLESSING OF THE BONFIRE (*ROMAN RITUAL*, CHAP. 2, NO. 16)

Priest: Our help is in the name of the Lord.

All: Who made heaven and earth.

Priest: The Lord be with you.

All: May he also be with you.

Priest: Let us pray. Lord God, almighty Father, the light that never fails and the source of all light, sanctify + this new fire, and grant that after the darkness of this life we may come unsullied to you who are light eternal; through Christ our Lord.

All: Amen.

The priest sprinkles the fire with holy water, and all sing the hymn Ut queant laxis.

Priest: There was a man sent from God.

All: Whose name was John.

Priest: Let us pray. God, who by reason of the birth of blessed John have made this day praiseworthy, give your people the grace of spiritual joy, and keep the hearts of your faithful fixed on the way that leads to everlasting salvation; through Christ our Lord.

All: Amen.

SAINTS PETER AND PAUL, APOSTLES (JUNE 29)

Saints Peter and Paul share this feast, as they are believed to have been martyred in Rome on the same day in AD 67: Saint Peter on the Vatican Hill, Saint Paul on the Laurentian Way.[24] Each seems an unlikely choice to lead the Church—one an illiterate fisherman who three times denied Christ, the other a Pharisaic tent maker who participated in the martyrdom of Saint Stephen (see John 18:15–18, 25–27; Acts 7:58). Yet Christianity without the legacy of either is unimaginable. Together they founded the Church in Rome, a city known then as the capital of the world and now as the "capital" of the Church.

Peter, "the prince of the apostles" and the first pope, ultimately affirmed his allegiance from his own personal cross. He requested to be crucified upside down, believing himself unworthy to die in precisely the same manner as his Lord. His body was buried under what is now the high altar of St. Peter's basilica in Rome.[25]

Paul's famous conversion on the way to Damascus turned him into an ardent supporter of the very Christians he had persecuted. As a Roman citizen he was spared the ignominious death on the cross and beheaded by sword. Archeology has confirmed very recently the burial of his body under what is now the Basilica of St. Paul Outside the Walls.[26]

EARLY MORNING SOLEMN ANGELUS

In rural Alpine regions, today starts early: The six o'clock morning Angelus is said outside, kneeling under garden trees. At the end of this solemn recitation, the people bow deeply, making the Sign of the Cross.

Tradition says that on this day, angels carry the apostolic blessing of the Holy Father throughout the world to all who sincerely await it. That being as it may, make your solemn Angelus an opportunity to pray for the Holy Father on the feast of his predecessor. If you say a decade of the rosary, use beads blessed by the pope or a bishop, as anyone who devoutly uses a religious object blessed by the pope or a bishop on this day and makes a profession of faith receives a plenary indulgence (no. 14, s. 1).

PRAYER TO THE HOLY APOSTLES PETER AND PAUL

A partial indulgence is granted any day for reciting this prayer (no. 20).

Holy apostles Peter and Paul, intercede for us.

Guard your people, who rely on the patronage of your apostles Peter and Paul, O Lord, and keep them under your continual protection. Through Christ our Lord. Amen.

PRAYER FOR THE POPE

The faithful who recite this prayer on any day receive a partial indulgence (no. 25, s. 1).

Leader: Let us pray for our Sovereign Pontiff N.

All: The Lord preserve him and give him life, and make him blessed upon the earth, and deliver him not to the will of his enemies.

SAINT THOMAS THE APOSTLE (JULY 3)

Saint Thomas, who did not believe in the Resurrection until he touched the wounds of the risen Christ (see John 20:24–29), was the apostle to India. Legend tells us that King

Gondofer hired this architect by training to build him a palace in the Roman style. Instead the apostle built up the Church, using the money for alms and—as he would explain to an enraged king—building him a *heavenly* palace.[27]

Thomas is the patron saint of architects, builders and the Indian, Sri Lankan and Bengali peoples. He was buried in Mylapore, India, in a church he had built close to the shore. Thomas is said to have promised that floodwaters would never rise as far as the church, and, indeed, they never have. Area residents used it as a haven during the disastrous tsunami of 2004.

The Feast of Saint Thomas was originally celebrated on December 21, coinciding with the winter solstice, the longest night of the year, representing the doubt of Thomas. Following the calendar reform of 1969, the feast was moved to July 3 to commemorate the anniversary of the translation of the saint's relics to Edessa. The change ended the popular traditions of Saint Thomas' day.

But, Thomas being an apostle and Sabitha being a Sri Lankan architect, we feel this feast deserves to be celebrated. Enjoy a refreshing Indian drink, mango *lhassi*. Try serving a whole Indian dinner if you're adventurous!

SABITHA'S MANGO *LHASSI* (SERVES 4)

- 1 mango, peeled and sliced, without seed
- 1/2 cup plain yogurt
- 1 cup milk
- sugar and cinnamon to taste

Combine ingredients in a blender until foamy. Serve cold. It's that easy!

SAINT JOHN VIANNEY (AUGUST 4)

Saint John Vianney, the Curé of Ars, is a reminder to us that all the saints magnify, not detract from, the glory of God. John Vianney struggled through seminary, barely able to learn the Latin in which he was to administer the sacraments. Unpromising, he was sent to pastor the town of Ars, a place almost completely secularized in the aftermath of the French Revolution.

Saint John Vianney poured himself out in ministry. He spent hours memorizing his sermons and hearing confessions. His fasting was so intense that his cheeks collapsed. Tormented at night by demons, Satan once hissed to him, "If there were two more men like you, France would be lost to me!"

A remarkable preacher and confessor, John Vianney is the patron saint of parish priests. Write a letter today to the priests you know, thanking them for the ministry and sacrifices of their lives. You might want to invite one or more of them for dinner.

SAINT DOMINIC (AUGUST 8)

Saint Dominic, a Spanish priest and the founder of the Dominican order, deeply loved our Lord, committing himself to preaching the gospel heroically. Before his birth his mother dreamt that she was pregnant with a dog carrying a torch in its mouth. At his baptism she noticed a star rising from his chest; the star became his symbol in art and resulted in his patronage of astronomers.

In life Dominic's fervor combined with the Latin pun *Domini cane* to create his nickname "the hound of the Lord." His love for truth spurred him to preach a successful drive against the Albigensian heresy, affirming the goodness of creation and the authority of the Church. He is said to have received a vision of Our Lady in which she gave him a garland of roses, asking him to pray the rosary. In fact, the Dominicans continued Dominic's deep devotion to Mary by spreading rosary devotion throughout the world.

To celebrate this saint doggedly devoted to preaching the Light of Truth, we suggest a flaming, tongue-shaped dessert. Admittedly it's less a custom and more something we made up, but it tastes good.

BANANAS FOSTER (SERVES 6)

- 6 bananas
- 4–6 tablespoons unsalted butter
- 1 cup brown sugar
- 2 shots crème de banana
- 3 shots rum
- long kitchen match or raw spaghetti noodle
- powdered cinnamon
- vanilla ice cream

Slice bananas into lengthwise halves; set aside. Heat butter and sugar in a frying pan over medium heat, stirring constantly, for about 5 minutes. Add crème de banana and rum, and cook for 3 minutes, stirring frequently. Add bananas and cook for a minute, being careful not to overcook.

Turn off the lights. Light the long kitchen match or spaghetti noodle, then touch the flame to the liqueur. Sprinkle cinnamon over the frying pan to create miniature fireworks. When the flames die out, serve over ice cream.

SAINT FRANCIS OF ASSISI (OCTOBER 4)

You doubtless have seen Saint Francis depicted preaching to flocks of birds or hugging animals, but this saint is just as often depicted alone, in the darkness, meditating on a human skull. Perhaps the preeminent "joyful saint," Francis was devoted to the passion of Christ, always contemplating it, always imitating it and ultimately being marked by a seraphim with the *stigmata*, the wounds of the Passion.[28] These two sides of Francis are deeply connected, showing us the path of a truly spiritual Christian.

Francis' is not a cheap spirituality that tries to be peaceful and happy by evading the hardships of the world. The saint shows us that peace and joy come not from the absence of hardship but from the firm embrace of the silence, the loneliness, the death we all face in this world. The emptiness drives us to seek our intimacy in Christ. In the complete devotion to Christ that comes from renouncing the pleasures of this world, Francis discovered a joy so deep and so attractive that his life became entirely illuminated by the love of the crucified Jesus.

Francis could weep at the sight of animals filling a stable to reenact the birth of Christ, and he could cry out in cosmic joy to "brother sun and sister moon"—all because, having stripped away earthly pleasures and having wrestled with the isolation of the human experience, he was able to embrace Christ alone, the hope of the nations. In honor of the saint who was so moved by the beauty of a world redeemed from pain and suffering by the death of Christ, many parishes offer the traditional blessing of animals today, found in the current *Book of Blessings*.

SAINTS SIMON AND JUDE (OCTOBER 28)

"Our parish is so bad we need two patron saints," joked the pastor of Sabitha's home parish. And what saints! After the Ascension the pair traveled together through Persia and Syria. Both were martyred, Saint Simon cut in half by a saw and Saint Jude beheaded after a beating.

Simon we know simply as "the Zealot," but Jude we know as the author of a New Testament book and patron saint of desperate causes (see Luke 6:15; Jude 1:1). Jude's symbol is a coin or medallion: this image is the *Mandylion* of Edessa, a miraculous image of our Lord that the apostle is believed, with surprising credibility, to have brought to King Abgar V of Edessa.[29]

The similarity of the name *Jude* to *Judas Iscariot* may lie behind the saint's patronage of desperate causes. Praying to Judas Iscariot would do no good, because the salvation of the one who betrayed Christ seemed an impossible cause. This connection inspired steady growth in the formerly minimal devotion to Jude Thaddeus. Even today messages of thanks to Saint Jude appear in the classifieds.

APOSTLE COOKIES

The apostles are the foundations of our Church, our vital connection to the person of Jesus, his teaching and his mandate to "make disciples of all nations, baptizing them" (Matthew 28:19). We therefore recommend that you celebrate all of their feasts, though not all the apostles have customs historically associated with them.

They all do have, however, traditional symbols. We therefore suggest "apostle cookies" as a way to celebrate the foundations of our Church's faith and structure.

Roll out a batch of cookie dough, either frozen or from scratch. Use a gingerbread man cookie cutter from your Christmas collection. Originally gingerbread men were spice cookies made in the image of Saint Nicholas, a bishop. Even today many gingerbread cookie cutters have a triangular hat, which is, in fact, Saint Nicholas's miter. Since the apostles were the first bishops, the miter—though an anachronism—is quite fitting.

Once your cookies are cut and baked, you can use the artistic symbols of the apostles to decorate them. The symbols are usually the means of their death, but don't let these gruesome implements of torture spoil your sweet tooth. Use red frosting to remind you of the sweetness of a martyr's love.

ALL SAINTS' AND ALL SOULS' DAYS (NOVEMBER 1 AND 2)

These feasts have their roots in the ancient Church at Antioch, where an annual feast in honor of all martyrs was celebrated the Sunday after Pentecost. By the seventh century this feast of all martyrs had spread throughout the entire Church, and it was celebrated in Rome on May 13. By 844 it

THE APOSTLES' SYMBOLS IN ART

Saint Philip (May 3): Because he was stoned and crucified against a pillar, stones, a pillar and a T-shaped cross on a crosier.

Saint James the Lesser (May 3): Son of Mary Cleophas, the Blessed Virgin's cousin. Because he was first bishop of Jerusalem, a miter. Because he was flung from the temple and beaten to death, the temple and a club.

Saint Matthias (May 14): Preached either in Judea or in Ethiopia. Because he was killed either by an axe (if you ask the Germans) or by spear (if you ask the Italians), these are his symbols.

Saint Peter (June 29): Because Christ gave him the keys to heaven, two keys (Matthew 16:19). Because he was the first pope, the papal tiara. Because he was crucified upside down, an upside-down cross.

Saint Paul (June 29): Both because he speaks of the Word of God as a sword and because, as a Roman citizen, he had a right to die by sword rather than crucifixion, a sword.

Saint Thomas (July 3): Because he was martyred in India by Brahmin priests, stones and a lance. Because he was trained as an architect, a builder's square.

Saint James the Greater (July 25): Because his tomb is the most famous shrine in Spain, the pilgrim's staff and the seashells pilgrims carry. Because he was beheaded, an axe—or break the heads off the cookies!

Saint Bartholomew (August 24): Because he was flayed in Armenia, a large knife.

Saint Matthew (September 21): Because he was a tax collector, a purse or bag, or the sword used to martyr him following his preaching in Egypt and Ethiopia.

Saint Simon (October 28): Martyred in Persia, the saw that cut him in two.

Saint Jude Thaddeus (October 28): Because he brought the *Mandylion* of Edessa, he holds a coin or medallion with the face of Christ.

Saint Andrew (November 30): Because he was a fisherman, fish. Because he went to Greece and was crucified, an X-shaped cross.

Saint John (December 27): Because he stayed close to the cross and shared Christ's sacrifice, though he was not martyred, use white frosting. Because he was forced to drink poisoned wine but lived, a chalice and serpent (see Mark 16:18). Because he was the youngest apostle, he is shown as beardless, and because by legend he lived to the age of ninety-nine, he is shown as an old man. Because he founded the seven churches of Asia Minor, a seven-candle candelabra (see Revelation 1:20).[30]

celebrated all the blessed, and it was transferred to November 1. In 1048 the Feast of All Souls was added.[31]

The reason for this transfer of All Saints' Day seems to be practical. So many pilgrims came to Rome for the festivities that the city would run out of food: The feast was therefore moved to follow the harvest.

Because a saint, or "holy one," is quite simply any soul that has attained the eternal bliss of heaven, there are millions more saints than the Church could ever commemorate. The Church sets aside All Saints' Day to honor, in the words of the old *Liber Pontificalis*, "all the apostles, martyrs, confessors, and all the just and perfect servants of God whose bodies rest throughout the whole world."[32]

The Church's faithful have ever been mindful of the bonds of charity that bind us to those holy souls who, though saved by Christ, await the complete purgation of their souls before appearing pure and holy before God (see Revelation 21:27). These souls, not yet able to enjoy the gift of heaven because they have not been liberated fully from their attachment to sinful tendencies, benefit from the prayers and invocations of the Church on their behalf (see 2 Maccabees 12:45). For this reason the Church has set aside the Feast of All Souls to pray for their complete deliverance. Pope Benedict XV granted priests the privilege of offering three Masses on this day, to emphasize the fact that by offering Christ's completed work of salvation to the Father, the suffering of the holy souls can be extinguished and their hearts at last fully immersed in God.

The placement of these feasts in November defined how people celebrated them. If your church, for example, had a summer picnic, it might look a lot like the Fourth of July, with fireworks, a barbecue and so on. That's how Americans celebrate in the summer. Europeans similarly kept November feasts in the way they knew to celebrate.

People used many pre-Christian autumnal customs in celebrating these new Christian feasts. The Celts had celebrated their dead in the beginning of November; they believed that souls, demons and spirits roamed the earth, and accordingly they left bread on the graves of their beloved and lit fires to help light their way or to scare them off. People left their doors open so that the dead might pass through—Lord knows you wouldn't want them stuck in your home. Because the demons played tricks on the living, the living could choose either to placate the spirits with sweet foods or to disguise themselves as spirits and join in the trickery.[33]

You will recognize this chaos in the current celebration of Halloween, or All Hallow's Eve. Children dress up as ghosts, demanding treats or threatening tricks, and adults light jack-o'-lanterns to guide or to scare away these tricksters. Some American Catholics, uncomfortable with the Druidic elements of Halloween, have All Saints' parties instead; that's what we did at Notre Dame. But if you would like to keep the scare in Halloween while making it slightly more Christian, *The Bad Catholic's Guide for Good Living* suggests holding a Purgatory Day party—which is scarier than ghost stories anyway.[34] Don't believe us? Read selections from *Purgatory: Explained by the Lives and Legends of the Saints* by Father F.X. Schouppe (Tan).

DÍA DE LOS MUERTOS

If you studied Mexican culture in Spanish class, you probably learned about *Día de los Muertos,* which entails All Souls' Day customs common to Catholic countries in Europe and the Americas. In the time leading up to All Souls', cemetery lawns were tended, graves were decorated with flowers, and funerary lanterns (*Seelenlichter*, or "Lights of the Holy Souls" in German) were placed at the headstones, waiting to be lit through All Souls' night. At nightfall all the lights were put out, except for the family's vigil candle, around which everyone gathered to offer prayers for departed family members.[35]

The Mexican custom is to build an elaborate altar, decorated with tissue paper, skulls made from sugar, flowers and pictures of deceased family members. The bread that in pagan times was left on the graves of the dead was made by Christians throughout Europe, known as *Seelenbrot* to the Germans and *Pan del Muertos* in Spanish. Unlike the pagans, Christians eat this bread on the feast or give it to the poor. Mexicans hold a picnic in the cemetery, cleaning the tombs, talking with friends, singing and eating late into the candlelit night. *Pan del Muertos* is served with one of the best drinks conceived by the human mind, Mexican *horchata*.

PAN DEL MUERTOS

- 5 cups flour
- 3 tablespoons leaven, such as baking powder
- 1 cup sugar
- a pinch of salt
- 5 eggs
- 5 egg yolks
- 1 cup margarine
- 1 tablespoon grated orange peel
- 3 tablespoons orange blossom water (in a pinch, regular water)

Mix the baking powder with 4 tablespoons of warm water, add 1/2 cup flour, and form a small ball of soft dough. Leave it 15 minutes in a warm place until it grows to twice its size.

Sift the remaining flour with the salt and sugar; form a heap and place in the middle 3 eggs, the 5 yolks, the margarine, the grated orange peel and the orange blossom water. Mix and knead well.

Add the small ball of dough. Knead again and let rest in a warm place for 1 hour. The dough should grow to almost twice its size again.

Knead again. Form the loaves of bread (usually shell-shaped) in the desired size, reserving some dough for decoration (see below), and place them in a greased pan.

Decorate the loaves with the shapes of bones and tears made of the same dough. Beat the 2 leftover eggs, and use them to paste the shapes on the loaves and to varnish the entire loaves. Sprinkle loaves with sugar.

Cook the bread in an oven preheated to 350 degrees, 30 to 40 minutes. Cool before serving.

SAINT ELIZABETH OF HUNGARY (NOVEMBER 17)

Raised a princess, Elizabeth married Prince Louis of Thuringia. Though this was an arranged political marriage, the couple loved each other deeply, and Louis was supportive of his wife's generosity to the poor. One day, as she was carrying bread to the poor, the prince asked what she had in her apron. Hoping to keep her charity concealed, she replied that she had roses. Louis asked her to open the apron, and roses fell out. Thus Saint Elizabeth is often pictured with her apron full of roses.[36]

After Louis' death in the Crusades, Elizabeth became a Franciscan tertiary. She lived in poverty, caring for the sick and dying. All this before her death at the age of twenty-four.[37]

Saint Elizabeth's Day is a good time to recognize the materially and spiritually poor among us. You might follow Elizabeth's example literally, bringing bread and roses to shut-ins or neighbors. Consider employing the Church's "Blessing for Bread in Honor of Any Saint," found in your parish's *Book of Blessings*. Sabitha and her best friend baked bread in a dorm kitchen between classes to hand out to hungry college students.

SAINT ELIZABETH'S BREAD (MAKES 15–20 ROLLS)

- 5 cups all purpose flour, sifted
- 2 packages rapid-rise yeast
- 1/4 cup sugar
- 1/4 cup honey
- 1/4 cup butter
- 2 tablespoons cinnamon
- 1 tablespoon nutmeg
- 2/3 cup milk
- 2 eggs, beaten
- 2 tablespoons butter, melted for glaze

Grease a 9 x 13-inch cake pan. Mix flour, yeast and sugar in a large mixing bowl. Heat honey, butter, cinnamon, nutmeg and milk until warm, about 40 seconds. Combine with flour mixture. Add eggs and knead on floured board until smooth, adding more flour or milk if needed.

Rub a bowl with butter and place dough inside, covered with a damp cloth. Leave in a warm place for 20 to 30 minutes. Knead again and divide into 4-inch balls.

To create a rose-shaped bread roll, roll a ball into 3 ropes, reserving a small amount. Braid the strands, and attach the ends to form a circle. Roll the reserved amount into a ball and place it in the middle of the circle.

Place the shaped rolls in the cake pan, and let them sit in a warm place 20 minutes. Bake at 350 degrees, 35 to 45 minutes, until golden. Just before the end of baking, glaze rolls with melted butter, then return them to the oven for a few minutes.

SAINT BARBARA (DECEMBER 4)

If Disney made a movie about the life of a saint, it would be Barbara. The daughter of a wealthy man named Dioscorus, Barbara was so beautiful that her father built a tall stone tower in which to hide her from the stream of princes who came to woo her. As the tower was being constructed, Barbara insisted that it have three windows in honor of the Holy Trinity, for Jesus Christ was her true love. Dioscorus, a fervent pagan, was so enraged that he eventually killed her.

In the Middle Ages Saints Barbara and Nicholas were two of the most popular saints, but Saint Barbara's feast went the way of Christopher's and Valentine's in the 1969 revision of the missal. At Mass most places commemorate Saint John of Damascus instead. Today is still officially Barbara's feast day, however, and she was never removed from the list of saints.

SAINT BARBARA'S TWIG (*BARBARAZWEIG*)

According to an ancient German custom, Saint Barbara spent her last days in the tower watering a twig from a cherry tree; the twig bloomed the day of her execution. You can bring home this custom by having each member of the family choose a thin branch with clear buds. If you are short on cherry branches, try apple, pear, peach, plum, lilac or any similar branch instead. Be sure to place a tag on each branch identifying the owner, place them all in a vase with water and then set the vase in a dark corner.

Some say that the person whose branch blossoms first will marry the following year; others say the person who has the most blossoms is "Mary's favorite," and that person might receive a special gift. Either way the flower born in dark of winter is a wonderful meditation on the coming of Christ, the Flower of heaven born into a bleak world marred by sin.

Place the blossoms on the family altar in front of the manger scene or on the dining table on Christmas Day, as Saint Barbara's offering to the Lord Jesus Christ, whom she so deeply loved.[38]

SAINT NICHOLAS (DECEMBER 6)

Saint Nicholas was born into a rich family, but with the death of his parents he determined to give his wealth to the poor. Stories of his charity inspired all of Christendom, fueling the saint's immense popularity.

According to legend, Nicholas's neighbor was on the verge of forcing his three daughters into prostitution due to extreme poverty. The saint threw a bag of gold into the neighbor's window for three nights, supplying each daughter in turn with a dowry.[39]

Nicholas became the bishop of Myra in Asia Minor. He was jailed under the Roman emperor Diocletian and released by Emperor Constantine, who legalized Christianity. Nicholas participated in the Council of Nicea, which defined the doctrine of the Holy Trinity and wrote the Nicene Creed. He died around 350 in his hometown of Myra.

Nicholas is the source of our modern "Santa Claus": he came every year the night before his feast to give gifts to children, as he had to his three neighbor girls. With the Reformation the Catholic bishop became the fat, jolly old elf known in historically Protestant countries such as England and, well, America. Ironically enough, Saint Nicholas was actually known for his extreme fasting. One author, generous to a historical fault, claimed that the baby Nicholas fasted from his mother's breast each Wednesday and Friday.[40]

A Visit From Saint Nicholas

Throughout Europe Saint Nicholas continues to visit children on his feast. Grandpa Salzmann's brothers and sisters always were amazed by this visit. A man dressed in episcopal regalia—miter and all—came to the homes of the parish children. The saint led the children in an Our Father before emptying his bags, handing out gifts to good children and advising naughty children. (Saint Nicholas carried a book in which guardian angels had made entries throughout the year, so he was well aware of each child's behavior.)

Saint Lucy and the demon Krampus sometimes accompanied Saint Nicholas, with Krampus rattling chains and threatening to grab hold of the chronically misbehaving. Perhaps some traditions are best left in Europe. Before leaving, the saint might give the whole family a quick sermon on the importance of preparing for the coming of Christ during this Advent season. Giving his blessing, he would depart.[41]

THE SHOES

The visit of Saint Nicholas could be a production difficulty for a household to pull off on its own (but, as Sabitha's Aunt Naomi has shown, not impossible). Instead, both Andrew's and Sabitha's families practiced the widespread custom of the shoes. When the children went to bed the night before Saint Nicholas Day, they put their shoes outside their bedroom doors. Just as he had in life, Saint Nicholas left his gifts in the dark of night—perhaps some candy, a Christmas ornament or a few holy cards.

A LETTER TO SAINT NICHOLAS

Saint Nicholas also gives Christmas letters from children to the Christ child, *Christkindl*, who in European tradition brings the gifts on Christmas Day. The children tell Jesus what sacrifices of prayer and fasting they plan to make throughout Advent and what they would like for Christmas. They place their letters on a windowsill on the eve of Saint Nicholas Day.

Some parents have used these letters as a means of behavior modification: very good children will have their letters delivered the first night, average children will have theirs delivered the second, and worse children may be forced to wait an agonizing three days or more.

SAINT NICHOLAS COOKIES

Many breads and cookies are made throughout Europe in the shape of Saint Nicholas. *Speculatius* or "image" cookies are printed with a mold. Usually sold in post-Reformation countries in the shape of windmills, finding the Christian version, imprinted with Saint Nicholas, takes some effort.

The classic gingerbread man is another secularized version of the Saint Nicholas cookie. Pull out the cookie cutters, and decorate your gingerbread as the saint they were intended to be.

- 1/2 cup corn syrup
- 3/4 cup light brown sugar
- 1/2 cup butter or margarine
- 1 whole egg
- 3/4 tablespoon cloves
- 3/4 tablespoon ginger
- 2 to 2-1/2 cups flour
- 1/2 tablespoon baking soda

On low heat, warm syrup, brown sugar and butter until the butter melts. When cool, mix in the egg, spices, flour and baking soda. Cover the dough with plastic wrap or wax paper, and let it rest overnight at room temperature.

The next day roll the dough quite thin, using flour to keep it from sticking to the board. Cut out the cookies, and bake in an oven at 350 to 375 degrees for 6 minutes. Decorate in an appropriately ecclesiastical manner.

SAINT LUCY (DECEMBER 13)

Saint Lucy suffered under the same emperor who persecuted Saint Nicholas, Diocletian. Born at Sicily in 283, she was the daughter of rich parents; unfortunately, her father passed away early in her life.

Lucy appears to have been inspired by the example of Saint Agatha, who had been martyred about fifty years prior while defending a vow of virginity in honor of Jesus Christ. Legend tells us that Lucy and her sick mother took a pilgrimage to the church housing the relics of Saint Agatha, and while praying before the relics Lucy's mother was cured.[42]

Lucy took the opportunity to request that her mother donate Lucy's inheritance to the poor—which provoked the ire of a man to whom she had been betrothed against her will. The greedy young man denounced Lucy as a Christian to the Roman governor, and she was killed in 303.

SAINT LUCY'S CROWN

During her life Lucy is supposed to have fed Christians hiding in the catacombs. She is said to have continued this type of provision posthumously. Following public prayers at Syracuse, Sicily, during the famine of 1582, the figure of Saint Lucy brought ships of grain into the harbors of Syracuse and Palermo. She was dressed in white, with a crown of candles on her head.

Less documented accounts claim that Saint Lucy fed the Swedes as well. At some unknown time in the past, during a severe winter famine, she was seen in white robes and halo bringing in a ship full of food over Lake Vänern, the largest lake in Sweden. Her feast day remains one of the highlights of the year in Sweden even today.

In commemorating the saint, a young girl dresses in a white gown, a crown of seven candles (more prudent modern Swedes substitute electric candles) and a red sash, symbolizing Lucy's martyrdom. The maiden comes bearing grain in the form of saffron buns, gingerbread cookies and coffee, followed by other children singing songs in honor of Lucy. The procession goes either from house to house or simply to the parents' bedroom for breakfast.

LUSSEKATTER (SAINT LUCY BUNS) (MAKES 24 BUNS)

- 1 tablespoon yeast
- 1/4 cup water
- 3/4 cup milk, lukewarm
- 1/3 cup sugar (divided)
- 1/4 cup melted butter
- 2 teaspoons turmeric powder
- 3 cups flour
- 1 teaspoon salt
- 1 egg, beaten
- 1 egg white for glaze

Dissolve the yeast in the water. Mix 1 tablespoon sugar with the milk, then add the yeast mixture and let proof 10 to 15 minutes.

In a small bowl stir the turmeric into the melted butter and reserve. In a large bowl sift together the flour, salt and remaining sugar. Add the proofed yeast mixture and egg. Stir until all the dry ingredients are incorporated.

Knead 5 to 7 minutes or until elastic. Place the dough in a lightly oiled bowl in a warm place to rise until doubled in size, about 1 hour and 15 minutes.

Lightly grease a cookie sheet. After the dough has risen, knead it gently for 30 seconds. Roll the dough into strands, and make S or figure-8 rolls, 3 to 4 inches long. Place the rolls on the cookie sheet and let rise again, about 1 1/2 hours.

Preheat oven to 350 degrees. Bake rolls for 15 minutes or until light gold. Brush with egg white, and return to the oven for a few minutes. Cool on a wire rack.

SONG TO SAINT LUCY

To the tune of "Are You Sleeping?"

> O Saint Lucy, O Saint Lucy
> Wearing white, wearing white,
> Lighting up the darkest, lighting up the darkest
> Winter night, winter night.

ADAM AND EVE (DECEMBER 24)

Yep, you read that right: Saint Adam and Saint Eve. The *Roman Martyrology* lists the day before the feast of the New Adam (Christ) as the feast of the original Adam (see 1 Corinthians 15:45).

You've repeated the innocuous phrase "He descended to the dead" countless times at Mass. The Church has always taught that, between Christ's death and resurrection, he led the souls of all the just who had lived before his coming (Abraham, Isaac, the prophets, Adam and Eve) through the newly opened gates of heaven. And so, while Genesis reports that Adam and Eve repented of their sin and continued to offer God sacrifice and praise, it was not until the saving work of Christ was complete that they entered into communion with God.

Paradise Tree

Christmas trees descend from medieval plays performed on the Feast of Adam and Eve. Known as a "Paradise tree," an evergreen was decorated to represent the Tree of Knowledge of Good and Evil.[43] The expulsion of Adam and Eve from the Garden of Eden was reenacted around it. The tree was decorated with red apples, signifying the forbidden fruit, but also with a promise of the redemption to come: cookies, signifying the Eucharist.

To celebrate the Feast of Adam and Eve, consider decorating your Paradise tree with its lights, apples and cookies this morning, and recall the expulsion from Paradise during the day. Add your Christmas decorations in the evening.

SAINT JOHN THE EVANGELIST (DECEMBER 27)

Saint John the evangelist is also Saint John the apostle: he is the only apostle said to have written a gospel. He is referred to as "the disciple whom Jesus loved" (John 21:20; see 13:23), and indeed our Lord entrusted Mary to John from the cross (suggesting that our Lord really was an only child). John is the only apostle, in fact, who did not run from Jesus during the Passion and crucifixion. Perhaps because he shared so deeply in Christ's passion, it was not necessary that he have his own: Saint John is the only apostle who was not martyred.

BLESSED WINE

According to legend, Saint John was given a cup of poisoned wine in an assassination attempt. When the apostle made the Sign of the Cross over the wine, the cup split in half, spilling the poisoned wine. In memory of this event, it became customary for priests to bless wine brought to church after Mass on this day. Bring a bottle to share tonight, but if a wedding is in your immediate future, follow another custom and have the bride and groom's bottle blessed today.[44]

BLESSING OF WINE ON SAINT JOHN'S DAY (ROMAN RITUAL, CHAP. 2, NO. 3)

Priest: Our help is in the name of the Lord.

All: Who made heaven and earth.

Priest: The Lord be with you.

All: May he also be with you.

Priest: Let us pray. If it please you, Lord God, bless + and consecrate + this vessel of wine (or other beverage) by the power of your right hand; and grant that, through the merits of Saint John, apostle and evangelist, all your faithful who drink of it may find it a help and a protection. As the blessed John drank the poisoned potion without any ill effects, so may all who today drink the blessed wine in his honor be delivered from poisoning and similar harmful things. And as they offer themselves body and soul to you, may they obtain pardon of all their sins; through Christ our Lord.

All: Amen.

Priest: Lord, bless + this creature drink, so that it may be a health-giving medicine to all who use it; and grant by your grace that all who taste of it may enjoy bodily and spiritual health in calling on your holy name; through Christ our Lord.

All: Amen.

Priest: May the blessing of almighty God, Father, Son, + and Holy Spirit, come on this wine (or other beverage) and remain always.

All: Amen.

The priest sprinkles the bottles with holy water.

"THE LOVE OF SAINT JOHN"

After being blessed, the wine is drunk before the family's main meal. Each person lifts his or her cup in the direction of another and says, "I drink to you the love of Saint John." That person responds, "I thank you for the love of Saint John." In a family setting this little ceremony is begun by the father and mother, then continues from one person to another.[45]

RECIPE FOR MULLED WINE

- 1 bottle blessed red wine
- 2 whole cloves
- 2 2-inch cinnamon sticks
- 1 vanilla bean
- 1/2 teaspoon nutmeg

Gently stir the spices into the wine in a large saucepan. Cook over medium heat for about 5 minutes. Strain the wine and serve it hot. Caution: If the wine boils it can become vinegar.

SAINT SYLVESTER (DECEMBER 31)

You knew this was coming since the first line of the chapter. Pope at the time of Constantine the Great, who legalized Christianity, Sylvester's reign came to symbolize peace and prosperity. Across Europe decadent and robust treats served on his feast reflected the peace enjoyed under his pontificate.

In Switzerland the Salzmanns made *kuchen*. Many German families eat the cake around nine o'clock in the evening, gathered around the infant Jesus in a little thanksgiving supper. The family can talk through the blessings and hardships of the year, thanking each other for their kindnesses and, above all, thanking our Lord.

You might round out this party by singing or reciting the Church's official hymn of thanksgiving, the *Te Deum*. If sung or recited publicly today, the Church grants participants a plenary indulgence (no. 26, s. 1). The hymn "Holy God, We Praise Thy Name" is loosely based on the *Te Deum;* you might want to sing this well-known version instead. However, the indulgence does not attach to this song.

SALZMANN RECIPE FOR APPLE *KUCHEN*

- 1 package active dry yeast
- 3/4 cup warm water (105–115 degrees)
- 3 tablespoons sugar
- 2 tablespoons vegetable oil
- 1/2 teaspoon salt
- 1 egg
- 2 cups flour
- 3 or 4 tart apples, peeled, cored and sliced in 1/2 inch wedges

- topping: 1 cup sugar and 3 tablespoons cinnamon

Make bread dough with first 7 ingredients and let rise once. Place bread dough in a 9 x 13-inch cake pan, and push down to cover the surface of the pan. Let the bread dough rise a second time while you prepare the apples.

Press the narrow parts of the apple wedges into the dough in rows, covering the entire surface. Sprinkle apples with the topping. Bake at 350 degrees. Serve warm.

SYLVESTER PUNCH: DON'T EAT THAT *KUCHEN* WITHOUT IT!

- blessed red burgundy (1 bottle for every 6 people)
- equal amount of hot tea
- 12 cloves
- rind of 1 lemon
- 2 tablespoons sugar to each bottle of wine
- 2 cinnamon sticks to each bottle of wine

Pour the wine into an enamel pot. Add the cloves, lemon rind, sugar and cinnamon. Heat over a low flame, but do not allow to boil. At the last moment add the tea. Serve hot.[46]

CELEBRATING OTHER SAINTS

So what about all the *other* days of the year? How will you satisfy your deep devotion to Saint Cunigunda? What about the feast of your Uncle David's patron saint, or how will you commemorate Saint Thérèse's day?

The official list of saints, and the days on which they are commemorated, is known as the *Roman Martyrology*. It's a wonderful resource, though entirely in Latin. Once you find a saint you need to celebrate, what to do?

If you're a priest, you can celebrate Mass in honor of any saint the *Martyrology* includes for that day. Otherwise, an unexpected dessert or bowl of ice cream is enough to make a party for anyone. Or a whole meal might be planned, with ethnic dishes from the saint's home country, a holy picture on the table and a couple candles.

You've probably already noticed certain patterns in popular piety: special breads, flowers and so on. Chapter fifty-nine of the current *Book of Blessings* allows your priest to bless any of these items in honor of any saint: invent your own popular customs. Hey, they started somewhere. Songs, whether invented for the occasion or taken from the liturgy, are always appropriate.

The most effective commemorations are inspired by an anecdote or theme from the saint's life. At Notre Dame our friends took a cue from the monasteries and remembered Saint Catherine of Siena with a play about her life. You might go bowling on the anniversary of the death of Bishop Fulton Sheen, who almost was kicked out of the seminary for bowling in the hallway.

And however you celebrate, of course, begin with prayer.

Notes

Introduction: Catholic and Loving It

1. See Scott Hahn, *Letter and Spirit: From Written Text to Living Word in the Liturgy* (New York: Doubleday, 2005), pp. 11–52.

2. See Nathan A. Barack, *The Jewish Way to Life* (Middle Village, N.Y.: Jonathan David, 1975), p. 137.

3. See Barack, pp. 50–51.

4. Wayne A. Meeks, *The First Urban Christians: The Social World of the Apostle Paul* (New Haven: Yale University Press, 2003), p. 163. See footnotes to 1 Corinthians 5:7–8 and 16:8 in *The New American Bible* (Confraternity of Christian Doctrine, 1986), pp. 1235, 1249.

5. Leonard Dinnerstein and David Reimers, *Ethnic Americans: A History of Immigration and Assimilation* (New York: Harper & Row, 1975), p. 33.

6. Xavier Rynne, *Letters from Vatican City: Vatican Council II (First Session): Background and Debates* (London: Faber and Faber, 1962), p. 111.

7. Rynne, p. 96.

8. Cardinal Joseph Ratzinger, *The Spirit of the Liturgy,* John Saward, trans. (San Francisco: Ignatius, 2000), pp. 201–202. See also *CCC*, 1676.

9. *Sacrosanctum Concilium,* Constitution on the Sacred Liturgy, no. 13, www.vatican.va.

10. Irenaeus of Lyon, *Adversus Haereses,* 4.11.2, *Ante-Nicene Fathers,* Alexander Roberts and James Donaldson, eds. (Peabody, Mass.: Hendrickson, 2004), vol. 1, p. 474.

11. As told to the authors by Capuchin Brother Leo Wollenweber, author of *Meet Solanus Casey: Spiritual Counselor and Wonder Worker* (Servant). Concluding quote is from Capuchin Father Ephrem Karwowski.

Chapter One: Catholic at Home

1. Maria Augusta Trapp, *Around the Year with the Trapp Family* (New York: Pantheon, 1955), p. 153.

2. Throughout this book we will refer to the 1952 *Rituale Romanum* (Roman Ritual). The blessings in that edition have been replaced by the 1989 *Rituale Romanum* (Book of Blessings). The 1952 edition contains many blessings that were omitted in the more recent edition. In two specific instances, the Congregation for Divine Worship and the Discipline of the Sacraments refers the faithful who wish to continue these customs to blessings found in the earlier edition. (See *Directory on Popular Piety and the Liturgy,* footnotes 200 and 309, www.vatican.va.) In that spirit, our book does the same for other blessings that continue to be of interest to Catholics. Quotes from Roman Ritual in this book are from Part XI unless otherwise noted.

3. "Holy Water," *The Catholic Encyclopedia*, vol. VII (New York: Robert Appleton, 1910), pp. 432–433.

4. "Holy Water Fonts," pp. 433–435.

5. See *Sacrosanctum Concilium*, no. 60.

6. Vatican II, *Lumen Gentium*, Dogmatic Constitution on the Church, no. 11, quoted in *CCC*, 2204 and by Pope John Paul II, *Familiaris Consortio*, Apostolic Exhortation on the Role of the Christian Family in the Modern World, no. 21, November 22, 1981, www.vatican.va.

7. Quoting the Chaplet of Divine Mercy, as given to Saint Faustina Kowalska.

8. Greg Dues, *Catholic Customs and Traditions: A Popular Guide* (Mystic, Conn.: Twenty-Third, 1993), p. 189.

9. Pope Paul VI, *Indulgentiarum Doctrina*, Apostolic Constitution on Indulgences, January 1, 1967, no. 1, www.papalencyclicals.net.

10. *Indulgentiarum Doctrina*, no. 5.

11. *Indulgentiarum Doctrina*, Transitional Norms.

12. Pope John Paul II, Message to the Carmelite Family, March 26, 2001, no. 6, www.vatican.va.

Chapter Two: Days, Weeks, Months

1. John R. Powers, *The Last Catholic in America* (New York: Saturday Review Press, 1973), pp. 101–104.

2. Tertullian, *De Corona*, no. 3, in Roberts and Donaldson, *Ante-Nicene Fathers,* vol. 3 (Peabody, Mass.: Hendrickson, 2004), pp. 94–95; see also *CCC*, 2157.

3. John Vianney, *Sermons of the Curé of Ars*, Una Morrissy, trans. (Fort Collins, Colo.: Roman Catholic Books, 1959), p. 174.

4. Vianney, pp. 174–175.

5. Pamela Moran, ed., *A Marian Prayer Book* (Ann Arbor, Mich.: Servant, 1991), pp. 242–243.

6. *Didache*, no. 8.2, in James A. Kleist, trans., *Ancient Christian Writers*, vol. 6 (Westminster, Md.: Newman, 1948), p. 17.

7. Pope John Paul II, *Ecclesia de Eucharistia,* Encyclical Letter on the Eucharist in Its Relationship to the Church, April 17, 2003, no. 11, www.vatican.va.

8. Francis Xavier Weiser, *Handbook of Christian Feasts and Customs* (New York: Harcourt, Brace and World, 1958), p. 29.

9. Canon Law Society of Great Britain and Ireland in association with the Canadian Canon Law Society, *The Canon Law: Letter and Spirit* (London: Geoffrey Chapman, 1995), p. 701.

10. Trapp, p. 196.

11. See Trapp, pp. 187–188.

12. Weiser, p. 16.

13. *The Raccolta* is a collection of the Church's prayers and devotions.

14. Père Binet, *The Divine Favors Granted to St. Joseph* (Rockville, Ill.: Tan, 1983), p. 14.

15. James Martin, ed., *Awake My Soul: Contemporary Catholics on Traditional Devotions* (Chicago: Loyola, 2004), pp. 150–151.

16. www.ewtn.com/devotionals/prayers/blsac4.htm.

17. *Manual of Indulgences: Norms and Grants*, translated into English from the fourth edition (1999) of *Enchiridion Indulgentiarum: Normae et Concessiones* (Washington, D.C.: USCCB, 2006) p. 62.

18. Martin, p. 2.

19. Pope Benedict XVI, Wednesday Audience, July 5, 2006, www.zenit.org.

20. Joseph Ratzinger, "Theological Commentary" on the message of Fatima (Rome: Congregation for the Doctrine of the Faith, 2000), www.vatican.va.

21. Pope John Paul II, *Rosarium Virginis Mariae*, Apostolic Letter on the Most Holy Rosary, October 16, 2002, no. 1.

22. *Rosarium Virginis Mariae*, no. 10.

23. F. X. Schouppe, *Purgatory: Explained by the Lives and Legends of the Saints* (Rockford, Ill.: Tan, 1986), p. 41.

24. Jacques Le Goff, *The Birth of Purgatory*, Arthur Goldhammer, trans. (Chicago: University of Chicago Press, 1986), p. 39.

25. Tertullian, *Adversus Marcionem*, 4.34, Roberts and Donaldson, vol. 3, p. 406.

26. Tertullian, *De Corona Militis*, 3.2–3, Roberts and Donaldson, vol. 3, pp. 94–95.

Chapter Three: Milestones

1. Henry Granjon, *Along the Rio Grande: A Pastoral Visit to Southwest New Mexico in 1902*, Michael Romero Taylor, ed. (Albuquerque: University of New Mexico Press, 1986), pp. 37–39, reprinted in Timothy Matovina and Gerald E. Poyo, *Presente! U.S. Latino Catholics from*

Colonial Origins to the Present (Maryknoll, N.Y.: Orbis, 2000), p. 86.

2. T.H. White, ed., *The Bestiary: A Book of Beasts* (New York: Putnam, 1960), p. 132.

3. Lumen Gentium, no. 11, in *Vatican Council II: The Conciliar and Post Conciliar Documents*, rev. ed., Austin Flannery, trans. (Northport, N.Y.: Costello, 1998), vol. 1, p. 362.

4. Bishop's Committee on the Liturgy, *Catholic Household Blessings & Prayers* (Washington, D.C.: USCCB, 1989), pp. 236–240. See also, United States Conference of Catholic Bishops, *Book of Blessings* (Collegeville, Minn.: Liturgical, 1989), pp. 195-214

5. Trapp, p. 248.

6. Sophie Hodorowicz Knab, *Polish Wedding Customs and Traditions* (New York: Hippocrene, 1997), p. 44.

7. Knab, pp. 85–91.

8. Timothy M. Matovina, "Marriage Celebrations in Mexican American Communities," *Liturgical Ministry*, Winter 1996, pp. 22–26; www.ewtn.com/library/family/house.txt.

9. As in poem by Sedulius Caelius, *Carmen paschale II*, nos. 28–31.

10. Directory of Popular Piety, no. 248, quoting Augustine, *In Iohannis Evangelium*, Tractate CXXIV, no. 5, www.vatican.va.

11. See Maria Augusta von Trapp, *The Story of the Trapp Family Singers* (New York: Perennial, 2002), p. 161.

12. James Hall, *Dictionary of Subjects and Symbols in Art* (London: John Murray, 2001), p. 305.

13. Pope Benedict XVI, Address at World Youth Day 2005 Welcoming Ceremony, Cologne Airport, August 18, 2005, www.vatican.va.

Chapter Four: Advent and Christmas

1. Trapp, *Around the Year with the Trapp Family*, p. 27.

2. Trapp, *Around the Year with the Trapp Family,* pp. 41–42.

3. White, p. 105.

4. Trapp, *Around the Year with the Trapp Family*, p. 56.

5. Proclamation of the Birth of Christ ©1988. United States Conference of Catholic Bishops. Used with permission. All rights reserved.

6. Editorial Staff, *Treasured Polish Recipes for Americans* (Minneapolis: Polanie, 2001), p. 162.

7. Ethel L. Urlin, Festivals, *Holy Days, and Saints' Days* (London: Simpkin, Marshall, Hamilton, Kent, 1915), p. 249.

8. Meredith Gould, *The Catholic Home: Celebrations and Traditions for Holidays, Feast Days, and Every Day* (New York: Doubleday, 2004), p. 31.

9. Weiser, p. 136.

10. Weiser, p. 136.

11. Weiser, pp. 138–139.

12. Johannes Quasten, Walter Burghardt, Thomas Lawler, eds., *Egeria: Diary of a Pilgrimage, Ancient Christian*

Writers: The Works of the Fathers in Translation, vol. 38 (New York: Newman, 1970), pp. 96–97.

13. Meredith Gould, *The Catholic Home* (New York: Doubleday, 2004), p. 50.

14. Urlin, p. 30.

15. Robert Herrick, *Songs of the Nativity*, William Henry Husk, ed. (London: John Camden Hotten, 1868), p. 159.

Chapter Five: Lent and Easter

1. Theodore the Studite, *On the Holy Icons*, Catharine Roth, trans. (Crestwood, N.Y.: St. Vladimir's, 1997), pp. 29–30.

2. Justin Martyr, "The First Apology of Justin," §LXVI, Roberts and Donaldson, *The Ante-Nicene Fathers*, vol. 1 (Peabody, Mass.: Hendrickson, 2004), p. 185.

3. Regis J. Flaherty, *Catholic Customs: A Fresh Look at Traditional Practices* (Ann Arbor, Mich.: Servant, 2002), p. 69.

4. Weiser, p. 193.

5. Urlin, p. 61.

6. Methodius, "Three Fragments on the Passion of Christ," Roberts and Donaldson, in *The Ante-Nicene Fathers*, vol. 6 (Peabody, Mass.: Hendrickson, 2004), p. 400.

7. Urlin, p. 63.

8. Hans Urs von Balthasar, *Mysterium Paschale: The Mystery of Easter*, Aidan Nichols, trans. (Edinburgh: T&T Clark, 1990), p. 176.

9. Francis Xavier Weiser, *The Easter Book* (New York: Harcourt and Brace, 1954), p. 137.

10. Augustine wrote, "He [God] judged it better to bring good out of evil, than to allow nothing evil to exist," in his *Enchiridion*, xxvii. John Rotelle, ed., *The Augustine Catechism: The Enchiridion on Faith, Hope, and Love*, Bruce Harbert, trans. (New York: New City, 1999), p. 58.

11. Gregory Nazianzen, "On the Death of His Father," Philip Schaff and Henry Wace, eds., *Nicene and Post-Nicene Fathers*, vol. 7 (Peabody, Mass.: Hendrickson, 2004), p. 263.

12. Preface for Easter Mass, James Socias, ed., *Daily Roman Missal* (Huntington, Ind.: Our Sunday Visitor, 1998), p. 609.

13. Urlin, p. 73.

14. Weiser, p. 220.

15. See Urlin, p. 81.

16. United States Conference of Catholic Bishops, *Book of Blessings*, p. 644.

17. *Treasured Polish Recipes for Americans*, p. 34.

18. *Treasured Polish Recipes for Americans*, p. 35.

19. With thanks to http://fooddownunder.com.

20. Weiser, p. 241.

21. Trapp, *Around the Year with the Trapp Family*, pp. 142–146.

Chapter Six: Feasts of Our Lady

1. Hugo Rahner, *Our Lady and the Church* (Bethesda, Md.: Zaccheus, 2004), back cover.

2. Rahner, p. 34.

3. John of Thessalonica, *On the Dormition of Mary: Early Patristic Homilies,* Brian E. Daley, trans. (Crestwood, N.Y.: St. Vladimir's, 1998), p. 67.

4. Weiser, *Handbook of Christian Feasts and Customs*, p. 286.

5. Weiser, *Handbook of Christian Feasts and Customs*, p. 290.

6. Rahner, p. 11.

7. W.F. Rohman, "Family Religious Customs Among German People," in Family Life Bureau, *Customs and Traditions of the Catholic Family* (Long Prairie, Minn.: Neumann, 1994), p. 29.

Chapter Seven: Feasts of Other Saints

1. Jacobus de Voragine, *The Golden Legend*, Granger Ryan and Helmut Ripperger, trans. (Salem, N.H.: Ayer, 1991), pp. 155–156.

2. *Book of Blessings*, p. 611.

3. Weiser, p. 322.

4. Weiser, p. 322.

5. Paula Manini, "Shaping Tradition: The Saint Joseph's Day Table Ritual," in David A. Taylor and John Alexander Williams, eds., *Old Ties, New Attachments: Italian-American Folklife in the West* (Washington, D.C.: Library of Congress, 1992), p. 164.

6. Kerri McCaffety, *St. Joseph Altars* (Gretna, La.: Pelican, 2003), p. 36.

7. Manini, p. 171.

8. McCaffety, p. 38; see also Nancy Verde Barr, *We Called It Macaroni: An American Heritage of Southern Italian Cooking* (New York: Knopf, 1996), p. 94.

9. McCaffety, p. 56.

10. Weiser, *Handbook of Christian Feasts and Customs*, p. 325.

11. de Voragine, p. 234.

12. Ernst Schuegraf, *Cooking with the Saints* (San Francisco: Ignatius, 2001), p. 114.

13. Urlin, p. 96.

14. Marguerite Ickis, *The Book of Festivals and Holidays the World Over* (New York: Dodd, Mead, 1970), pp. 82–83.

15. Hall, pp. 199–200; see also Omer Englebert, *The Lives of the Saints*, Christopher and Anne Fremantle, trans. (New York: Barnes and Noble, 1994), pp. 159–160.

16. Fernando and Gioia Lanzi, *Saints and Their Symbols: Recognizing Saints in Art and in Popular Images*, Matthew J. O'Connell, trans. (Collegeville, Minn.: Liturgical, 2003), p. 72.

17. Lanzi, p. 72.

18. Schuegraf, p. 202.

19. Lanzi, p. 155.

20. Helen Walker Homan, *St. Anthony and the Christ Child* (New York: Farrar, Straus & Cudahy, 1958), pp. 180–181.

21. Augustine, Sermon 292, quoted in Weiser, p. 328.

22. Louis Bouyer, *Liturgical Piety* (Notre Dame, Ind.: University of Notre Dame Press, 1978), p. 227.

23. Weiser, p. 330.

24. Lanzi, p. 61.

25. Bernard Strasser, *With Christ through the Year: The Liturgical Year in Word and Symbols* (Milwaukee: Bruce, 1947), pp. 271–273.

26. Lanzi, p. 61; see also Strasser, pp. 273–274.

27. de Voragine, pp. 39–40.

28. Englebert, p. 378.

29. Liz Trotta, *Jude: A Pilgrimage to the Saint of the Last Resort* (New York: Harper Collins, 1998), pp. 118–120.

30. Major Arthur de Bles, *How to Distinguish the Saints in Art by Their Costumes, Symbols, and Attributes* (New York: Art Culture, 1925), pp. 56–59.

31. Weiser, pp. 307–309.

32. Louis Duchesne, ed., *Liber Pontificalis* (Paris, 1884–1892), vol. 1, p. 417, www.catholicculture.org.

33. Weiser, p. 315.

34. John Zmirak and Denise Matychowiak, *The Bad Catholic's Guide to Good Living* (New York: Crossroads, 2005), p. 175.

35. Weiser, pp. 310–311.

36. Joan Carroll Cruz, *Secular Saints: 250 Canonized and Beatified Lay Men, Women and Children* (Rockford, Ill.: Tan, 1989), p. 211.

37. Schuegraf, p. 84.

38. Bernard Stokes, *How to Make Your House a Home* (Washington: Family Life Bureau, 1955), p. 9.

39. de Voragine, p. 17.

40. de Voragine, p. 17.

41. Trapp, *Around the Year with the Trapp Family*, p. 31.

42. de Voragine, p. 34.

43. Weiser, p. 99.

44. Strasser, p. 85.

45. Trapp, *Around the Year with the Trapp Family*, p. 64.

46. Trapp, *Around the Year with the Trapp Family*, p. 69.